JANE ADDAMS

JANE ADDAMS

The Most Dangerous Woman
in America

Marlene Targ Brill

BIOGRAPHIES FOR YOUNG READERS

Ohio University Press
Athens

Ohio University Press, Athens, Ohio 45701
ohioswallow.com
© 2024 by Marlene Targ Brill
All rights reserved

To obtain permission to quote, reprint, or otherwise reproduce or distribute
material from Ohio University Press publications, please contact our rights and
permissions department at (740) 593-1154 or (740) 593-4536 (fax).

Printed in the United States of America
Ohio University Press books are printed on acid-free paper ∞ ™

Library of Congress Cataloging-in-Publication Data
Names: Brill, Marlene Targ, author.
Title: Jane Addams : the most dangerous woman in America / Marlene Targ
   Brill.
Description: Athens : Ohio University Press, [2024] | Series: Biographies for
   young readers | Includes bibliographical references. | Audience: Ages 8+ |
   Audience: Grades 4–6
Identifiers: LCCN 2024004544 (print) | LCCN 2024004545 (ebook) | ISBN
   9780821425527 (hardback) | ISBN 9780821425534 (paperback) | ISBN
   9780821425541 (pdf)
Subjects: LCSH: Addams, Jane, 1860–1935—Juvenile literature. | Women social
   reformers—United States—Biography—Juvenile literature. | Social ser-
   vice—Illinois—Chicago—History—Juvenile literature. | BISAC: JUVENILE
   NONFICTION / Biography & Autobiography / Social Activists | JUVENILE
   NONFICTION / History / Modern
Classification: LCC HV4196.C4 A3 2024 (print) | LCC HV4196.C4 (ebook) |
   DDC 361.92 [B]—dc23/eng/20240205
LC record available at https://lccn.loc.gov/2024004544
LC ebook record available at https://lccn.loc.gov/2024004545

Contents

Author's Note

As a child I was told I could enter any profession—within limits. At first I believed what I was told. But questions nagged at me.

In the 1950s, girls always wore skirts to school, even on the coldest winter days. *Why?* I asked. Boys didn't. Girls heard that they should be teachers, nurses, or secretaries, which are all fine professions. But I wanted to be an artist or a scientist. My mother, like many mothers, encouraged me to take typing class in high school as a backup to whatever profession I ultimately chose. Without computers in our vision, I wondered *Why typing?* I didn't see office work in my future.

Although many of my friends also thought of becoming something else, they didn't find colleges welcoming. Girls had few role models for working outside the home. Boys saw male presidents and doctors and lawyers and business executives all around them.

Teachers in the 1950s and 1960s fed students a constant diet of how the United States was founded on liberty and justice for all.

But the more history I studied, I discovered how life could be different. I read about a woman who founded a settlement house in Chicago called Hull-House. She helped the poor, improving their work and home lives. At the same time, she fought for women's right to vote and for world peace. Her name was Jane Addams.

During the late 1800s when Jane grew up, she experienced rough times because she was a girl. Unless she belonged to a farming or pioneer family or her family was poor—which required women to work outside the house for survival—a woman's place was firmly in the home.

Even into the twentieth century many American states still followed English common law. Under these laws, a father's word—and later a husband's word—was final. Women who married surrendered all rights to their husbands. They could not own property or sign contracts. Their husbands owned their clothes, the household goods, and anything they brought into the marriage. If a woman earned wages, the money belonged to her husband. Divorce was almost impossible. When a husband died, his wife could lose everything unless the man wrote a will detailing what she should receive. Even with a will, most states limited a woman to only one-third of her husband's holdings. After visiting the United States in 1831, French author Alexis de Tocqueville wrote, "No people, with the exception of slaves, had less rights over themselves in . . . America than married women."[1]

Religion further bound a woman to her husband. "Thy desire shall be to thy husband, and he shall rule over thee," said the Bible.[2] Both the laws and the church defined a woman's place, and the lack of higher education helped keep her there. Most fathers saw no need for daughters to receive more than basic education, if that much. With few exceptions, girls were raised to be good daughters, sisters, wives, and mothers.

Worst of all, women could not vote. Without a voice through voting, women had no say in laws affecting them. They had to be extra brave and smart, like Jane Addams, to make any changes.

Finding Jane motivated me to keep asking questions. She taught me that bucking the social norms of my day, just as she bucked hers, is a good thing. Jane stuck her nose into everything to make a better world. She went from a girl raised to follow rules to one of the most famous women in the world. She founded a settlement house, established worldwide peace organizations, and won the Nobel Peace Prize. At the same time, she ruffled political feathers, hounded three presidents, and pushed the rights of women to new heights. She lived life as she wanted for herself and for others.

Most men disliked being challenged by a woman. They branded any woman who spoke out as "dangerous." Eventually, Jane earned that title too. To me, being dangerous is a badge of honor. See what you think about all that Dangerous Jane accomplished.

JANE ADDAMS

ONE

SETTING THE STAGE FOR MUCH-NEEDED MISCHIEF MAKING

Action indeed is the sole medium of expression for ethics.

—Jane Addams

I N 1889 Jane Addams achieved her first notable accomplishment. Other achievements would follow. But this first project is what peo ple most commonly remember her for to this day.

Jane and her college friend Ellen Gates Starr, two fearless women, opened a community center in Chicago's Near West Side that became a place for the less fortunate to gather. The women called it a settlement house, one of the first in the United States. As Jane put it, "The Settlement is an experimental effort to aid in the solution of the social and industrial problems which [grow from] modern conditions of life in a great city."[1] Unlike most community centers, volunteers lived, or "settled," among the poor people they served. The venture turned out to be a grand social experiment. But it wasn't easy.

CHICAGO IN THE LATE 1800S

Chicago in the late nineteenth century was ripe for social change. As a relatively new midwestern transportation and communication hub, the city attracted industry at a rapid rate. The cross-country railroad system was built between 1867 and 1877. These large railroads came together with smaller lines in Chicago and encouraged the city's business growth.

Travelers and settlers found railroad transportation better than ox-drawn wagons or horseback. Industrialists in the northeast part of the nation invested in railroads as a new, cheaper method to transport their goods during the country's rapid expansion. Similarly, shipping increased on Chicago's two waterways: Lake Michigan and the Illinois and Michigan Canal. The city's midwestern location created a jumping-off spot for westward travel at a time when pioneers were exploring and settling lands that were new to White Americans.

Transportation opened Chicago to new industries, and the economy sizzled. Huge factory complexes sprang up, particularly on the city's south and west sides. These factories produced everything from salt to mattresses, musical instruments, and clothing. Steel mills supplied valuable materials for industry but also polluted the south side. A trademark smell blew from the Near West Side stockyards, where livestock were slaughtered, packed, and shipped nationwide more cheaply and quickly than ever before. Prairie farmers brought corn, wheat, and other farm products to Chicago for processing and shipping. By the early 1900s so many candy companies opened in Chicago that the city earned the name Candy Capital of the World.

Business groups such as the National Confectionary Association sprang up to **lobby,** or influence, politicians to aid them in building their companies. A wealthy class developed in Chicago to rival the captains of industry in the large cities of the eastern United States.

But not everyone benefited equally. Manufacturers claimed that they improved the lives of workers. By requiring long hours of labor, bosses felt that they helped fill idle time that otherwise would have been wasted. Most factory workers toiled ten to fourteen hours a day. They often started work before sunup and left only at sundown.

Greedy manufacturers paid employees low wages to increase profits but did nothing to prevent workers from having to live and work in run-down, dangerous, unhealthy conditions.

As the city grew, populations in the neighborhoods surrounding factories exploded. Migrants flocked to midwestern industrial centers, especially Chicago, from rural areas. Farming remained the top choice of labor in the US, but big industrial cities like Chicago lured workers from the countryside with promises of higher wages. But low pay, long work hours, and poor living conditions prevented most workers from getting ahead.

After the Civil War (1861–65), many formerly enslaved people in the South heard stories of thriving factory jobs and a better life in northern cities. A steady stream of migrants arrived in Chicago only to have their dreams dashed. Add to these migrants the farmers who longed for city life, and the number of jobs could not keep up with the multitudes who arrived to find work. Low pay along with poor, overcrowded living conditions resulted.

Immigration to the United States from foreign countries also affected Chicago. Between 1860 and 1900 the US population soared. The number of immigrants coming through New York's Ellis Island, the main entryway into the United States, more than tripled. After gaining entry in New York, a sizable group of immigrants traveled to expanding cities, such as Chicago, Saint Louis, Boston, and Philadelphia. These cities doubled their populations. By the time Hull-House opened, Chicago had grown to almost 1.7 million people. The city became the state's largest—and the nation's third most populous—city.

During the late 1800s immigrants from European countries like Germany, Ireland, Italy, Lithuania, and Poland came to the United States for a host of reasons. Some wanted jobs and a chance for a better life. Unskilled workers sought work in steel mills, stockyards, and meatpacking plants. Many others fled harsh governments that persecuted followers of certain religions, such as Roman Catholics and Jews.

Generations of immigrants, like this Italian family, crammed into small tenement apartments in Chicago.

National Archives

Newcomers willingly, at least at first, accepted low-paying and dangerous jobs. Lacking English language skills, many new immigrants preferred to live where people from their homelands already resided. They often crowded into neighborhoods near their workplaces. The area around Hull-House and the nearby Back of the Yards neighborhood teemed with Poles, Germans, and many Jews from Russia and Eastern Europe.

As the population skyrocketed, city transportation and communication improved. People with enough money moved to the more pleasant outer edges of the city. Pockets of mansions for the wealthy grew along Lake Michigan's tree-lined shores. This left poor families crowded into unsanitary and polluted industrial areas of the city's center. While "density where Hull-House sat (Nineteenth Ward) was 92 people per acre in 1890, newly created areas on the city's edges boasted one or two people per acre."[2]

MEETING ELLEN GATES STAR

Jane first met Ellen Gates Starr in 1849 during their first year in college. The two became instant friends. Both came from small towns—Jane from Cedarville and Ellen from Laona, Illinois. Ellen's father instilled in her a strong sense of social responsibility and fairness for all. Her aunt pushed for her education. These experiences were similar to Jane's as a girl.

Jane admired Ellen's strong religious faith and artistic talent. She loved Ellen's emphasis on beauty, something that fit with Jane's love of nature. The women stayed close even after Ellen left college at the end of their first year. Money was tight for Ellen, so she had to leave to teach school and earn a living. She first taught in Mount Morris, Illinois, before finding a better-paying job with Chicago Public Schools.

Slight Ellen Gates Starr became a force in labor reform, the arts, and literature.

Library of Congress

Ellen and Jane complemented each other. While Jane had a head for business, Ellen was lively and intense, like an artist. At Hull-House, Ellen focused on art and art education classes. She opened Chicago's first public art gallery and developed an art lending library with Chicago Public Schools. Her efforts led to the first arts education program at the Art Institute of Chicago.

Ellen believed that harsh working conditions and child labor crushed the creativity in these workers that she enjoyed. Therefore, she extended her activities to labor reform. She marched in protests for higher wages and against police cruelty. After joining the garment workers' job walkout, Ellen helped found the Women's Trade **Union** League in 1904. In 1914 she was arrested for what police said was disorderly conduct while marching with employees protesting conditions at Henrici's restaurant. She dared to tell the police to leave the marchers alone. Even at only one hundred pounds, Ellen could be powerful.

In early 1889 Jane and Ellen searched for the perfect place in the right neighborhood to open a settlement house, a place where they could offer education and culture to their poor and immigrant neighbors. They found a large but decaying mansion at 800 South Halsted Street on Chicago's west side. The building sat on one acre of land, large enough for expansion. They rented the house from Helen Culver, who had inherited the land from her cousin, original owner Charles Hull.

Hull, a real estate developer, originally built the house for himself in 1856 when the neighborhood was fashionable and flourishing. He originally planned to build more residences surrounding his newly built Italian-style mansion. But as Chicago expanded and grew more industrial, the neighborhood declined, becoming overcrowded, noisy, and smelly. Hull never developed the land, and after he died in early 1889, the mansion fell into disrepair. A saloon and a funeral parlor thrived on either side of the once-elegant home. By then, factories and slums surrounded the home. The entire area became neglected. Jane wrote, "The streets are inexpressibly dirty, the number of schools inadequate, [the cleanliness laws] unenforced, the street lighting bad, the paving miserable and altogether lacking in the alleys and smaller streets, and the stables foul beyond description."[3]

Jane saw possibilities there that no one else did, and the two friends got to work. Wide entrance halls and open fireplaces gave the house a welcoming feel. They bought new furniture and polished the woodwork. They decorated the rooms with items they had purchased while traveling overseas. The women happily did most of the work themselves to save money. They called their new home Hull-House after the original owner.

Jane was so enthusiastic and confident about her vision that Helen Culver agreed to support their work. She offered to provide the mansion and surrounding land rent free for four years. This donation allowed the doors to open while the women sought other funding. As the settlement house began to thrive, Culver permanently donated the land to Jane and Ellen for free.

Jane Addams modeled her Hull-House office after her childhood home.
Permission from Rockford University

Although the settlement house movement was in its infancy, especially in the United States, Jane envisioned endless possibilities for the people she and Ellen hoped to serve. In addition to assisting neighbors, Jane saw Hull-House as a center for people interested in developing new ideas. The profession of social work did not exist yet, so people who wanted to help improve the lives of others found nowhere to turn. At Hull-House like-minded people interested in social service could serve, support, and learn from each other. The one thing they had in common—besides their commitment to improving the lives of impoverished families—was where they resided and sharpened their community activist skills. Jane was their inspiration and leader.

The doors officially opened on September 18, 1889. From the beginning, Jane and Ellen emphasized that Hull-House should be guided by democracy for all, fellowship, and social service in the Christian spirit. Most settlement house founders emphasized some religion or other at their centers. Jane, however, sought to keep religion out of the project, despite her mention of Christ in the principles. She merely wanted a home that reflected the principles of social service, love, and human connection that she had experienced in her Christian upbringing. Her settlement house would be free of organized religion. It would be for everyone, regardless of nationality and religion, a safe place for all.

What gave Jane the strength and determination to tackle the city's—and later the world's—most pressing problems? As with most people, the answer lies in a mix of upbringing, bravery, and inner faith.

Did You Know?

During the 1800s, a worldwide movement of college-educated people sprang up to help the poor. This new thinking involved living among the poor and researching ways to improve their communities. Jane's inspiration for Hull-House was Toynbee Hall, London's first long-term settlement house. Thanks to successes at Hull-House, settlements caught on in the United States. Eventually, more than five hundred settlements dotted the US, with forty-three in Chicago alone. Many still exist today, but others now are called community centers.

TWO

NOT YOUR TRADITIONAL GIRL

Worthy old nature! She goes on producing whatever is needful in each season . . . even as she feeds
and nourishes her children. . . . [to] make them
wise and learned.

—Jane Addams

Laura Jane Addams was born in Cedarville, Illinois, on September 6, 1860. She was the eighth of nine children born to Sarah
Weber and John Huy Addams. Early in life and into her teens, everyone called her Jennie, which the family seemed to prefer.

Jane's full given name came from a beloved Cedarville teacher,
Laura Jane Forbes. Laura Jane taught at Cedarville Academy, the
elementary school founded by John Addams. As was often the custom
at the time, teachers lived with different families as part of their job
benefits. Forbes stayed a while with the Addams family and made a
favorable impression on them.

The spelling of Jane's last name had curious origins too. According to family lore, John's ancestors had arrived from England decades
earlier with only one *d* in their name. But one Adams ancestor, a cap-
tain during the Revolutionary War (1775–83), added the second *d* "to
avoid confusion with a cousin."[1] In fun, Abraham Lincoln, who served
with John Addams in the Illinois legislature, used to write his friend
letters addressed to "My dear double-D'd Addams."[2]

Jane's father, John Addams.
Courtesy of Rockford University

Jane's mother, Sarah Weber Addams.
Courtesy of the Swarthmore College Peace Collection

FAMILY BEGINNINGS

John, age twenty-one, and Sarah, age twenty-six, met and married in 1844 in Kreidersville, Pennsylvania. String-bean-tall John was a serious, plainspoken man. He projected a strong sense of duty and moral beliefs that valued education.[3] John had trained as a miller and was operating a flour mill by the time he met his future bride. Sarah came from wealth, so her family had sent her to boarding school. There she developed talents in languages, literature, and music. Those who knew her thought she was kindhearted and always ready to help anyone in need.

After they married, John decided that the new couple should head west. He knew some friends and family who had moved to Freeport,

Illinois. After traveling to northern Illinois by train, steamboat, and horse-drawn wagon, they landed in Cedar Creek Mills (later Cedarville), a small wooded village on the banks of Cedar Creek. The couple found no post office, school, church, or store. But the landscape reminded John of Pennsylvania, so he declared it "a fine site for a town."[4] His first task was to buy land uphill from the creek and to plant the Norway pine seeds he had carried from his home state.

John had vision and a strong work ethic. Not long after arriving, the twenty-two-year-old bought the Cedar Creek Grain Mill. He first built a small home, a two-room log cabin with a dirt floor. He figured that this size would hold them until he could construct something grander. Sarah wrote relatives back home: "You would no doubt laugh [to] see us in our 'log cabin 8' by 10' which serves for Parlour, Bedroom, Dining Room, & Kitchen."[5]

Within a few years, children filled the tiny cabin. With limited healthcare choices in those days, only five of the nine children lived beyond the age of two. Jane had three living older sisters: Mary was thoughtful like her mother and was considered the family beauty. Martha later died of **typhoid fever** at age sixteen. Sarah Alice (known as Alice) was the high-spirited, hot-tempered, and difficult member of the clan. Her older brother, John Weber (known as Weber), was the only of her brothers to reach adulthood.

Most of the siblings were at school or married by the time Jane was born. By then, John had built a large, brick home at the village's north end near a forest, orchard, and creek. The mansion earned the simple name "The Homestead."

Jane wrote in her first book, *Twenty Years at Hull-House*, that her earliest memory was a sad and meaningful story about her mother. At the time, Jane was little more than two years old but advanced for her age. People viewed her mother as a tough woman who was devoted to her family. Still, she had "a heart ever alive to the wants of the poor."[6] Her desire to promote good works was legendary among the community. But each of her pregnancies left her with a little less energy. In January 1863 forty-six-year-old Sarah was close to bearing her ninth

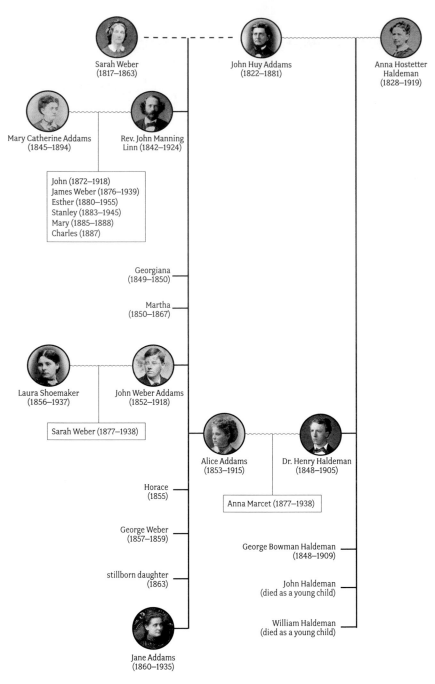

Sarah Weber (1817–1863)

John Huy Addams (1822–1881)

Anna Hostetter Haldeman (1828–1919)

Mary Catherine Addams (1845–1894)

Rev. John Manning Linn (1842–1924)

John (1872–1918)
James Weber (1876–1939)
Esther (1880–1955)
Stanley (1883–1945)
Mary (1885–1888)
Charles (1887)

Georgiana (1849–1850)

Martha (1850–1867)

Laura Shoemaker (1856–1937)

John Weber Addams (1852–1918)

Sarah Weber (1877–1938)

Alice Addams (1853–1915)

Dr. Henry Haldeman (1848–1905)

Anna Marcet (1877–1938)

Horace (1855)

George Weber (1857–1859)

George Bowman Haldeman (1848–1909)

stillborn daughter (1863)

John Haldeman (died as a young child)

William Haldeman (died as a young child)

Jane Addams (1860–1935)

Addams Family Tree that sprouted many branches.

Courtesy of Jim Bade, Cedarville Area Historical Society

The Homestead, Jane's childhood home.
Courtesy of the Cedarville Area Historical Society

baby. Yet she felt compelled to assist the wagonmaker's wife with her own troubled delivery. By the time a doctor arrived to tend the neighbor, Sarah had grown so exhausted that she collapsed.

Jane later wrote that she remembered hearing her mother's voice in the ground-floor bedroom of the house and wanting to see her. The child pounded on the door until she heard her mother call, "Let her in, she is only a baby herself."[7] Jane was allowed to stay with her mother as she slowly slipped away. The baby died, and Sarah Addams died afterward, on January 14, 1863.

Each family member experienced their grief in different ways. But talking about sadness wasn't how they operated. John buried himself in his work. He often stayed away for business. His children reacted according to their different personalities. Weber's grief triggered mental breakdowns that reappeared throughout his life, resulting in repeated stays in mental institutions. Martha resumed her schooling. Mary, the loving caretaker, returned from college to attend to Jane and the home for six years. Later, Mary and Alice chose horrible mates that resulted in unhappy marriages.

Mary Addams, Jane's sister who cared for her after their mother died.

Courtesy of the Swarthmore College Peace Collection

John Weber Addams, Jane's brother.

Courtesy of the Swarthmore College Peace Collection

Alice Addams (Sarah), Jane's other sister.

Courtesy of the Swarthmore College Peace Collection

Jane seemed little affected, but that was an illusion. She later wrote that her mother's death was "that mysterious injustice of life, the burden of which we are all forced to bear."[8] As a result, Jane grew unusually attached to her attentive but strict father. From an early age she developed a strong moral code, much like his. An insightful and thoughtful child naturally, she incorporated her mother's commitment to the poor with her father's strong feelings about nonviolence and equal rights.

DADDY'S GIRL

John became the strongest influence in Jane's life. Jane gave him all her affection. He was the person she most wanted to please. His word was law in the household, but he had a kind side that he rarely showed. That meant following his morals, which sometimes could be extremely strict. On one occasion, John ordered Jane to change from a new cloak into an old one. He believed that if someone wore better clothes, it might make other little girls feel bad. He thought that wearing fancier clothes decreased equality, even close to home.

John's energy knew no bounds. He maintained a strict daily ritual from his early days as a miller, rising at three o'clock in the morning. To please her father, Jane did the same. She used the extra morning time to

Earliest known photo of a sad-looking Jane at about four years old.

Courtesy of the Swarthmore College Peace Collection

read all the books in her father's library, just as he had done. John encouraged her reading. He offered Jane a nickel for every book she read and could explain to him.

John became a pillar of the community. Everyone looked up to him for his talents, honesty, and business skills. John was also the wealthiest man in the county. In addition to his flour mill, he owned a sawmill and a carriage factory. When he saw that the community needed something, he acted. After buying up most town businesses, he founded Second National Bank in Fremont.

John offered the same opportunities for people of all races and religions. He hated slavery. Before the Civil War, John had turned The Homestead into a stop along the **Underground Railroad**, the network of safe houses where escaping slaves could find shelter on their way to freedom farther north. He followed world news and sided with those less fortunate than himself.

Even though he claimed no religion, he helped establish the city's first Presbyterian church. He also founded the local school and opened his home library to villagers. At age thirty-two, he was elected to the state senate as a member of the Whig party. The party's antislavery members later split off and established the Republican Party in the 1850s. In Springfield, where John served in state government from 1854 through 1870, he earned a reputation for being the only state official never offered a bribe. His nickname, Honest John Addams, reflected the common knowledge that he would never accept one.[9]

Jane adopted her father's honest ways. She felt extreme guilt at the thought of telling a lie. As a young child she often had nightmares involving death and going to hell after she told a lie. She wrote in her autobiography, "My only method of obtaining relief was to go downstairs to my father's room and make full confession." Upon hearing the confession, John, to his credit, assured his terrified daughter that "if he had a little girl who told lies he was very glad that she felt too bad to go to sleep afterward."[10] To his mind, the fact that she was able to admit being wrong was enough to allow him to forgive his daughter's guilt.

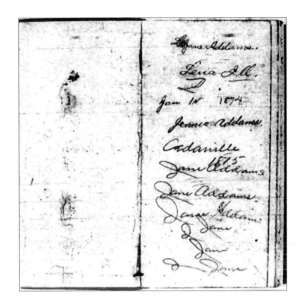

Jane practiced in her diary how she wanted her name to look.

Courtesy of Rockford University

Another much-quoted incident influenced Jane's thinking. One day she accompanied her father to a different town on mill business. For the sensitive seven-year-old, the trip proved life-changing. On past visits Jane had enjoyed the city's quaint homes and candy and toy shops. On this visit, though, John drove through shabby streets lined with tiny, cramped houses. Jane asked her father how people could live on top of one another like that. After all, she loved the forest and orchard surrounding her home. He explained that this was how poor people often lived. After listening carefully, Jane promised she would one day build a large house in the middle of horrible houses. That way, she could provide relief for her neighbors.

This goal was unusual for someone so young, but it was a promise that Jane ultimately kept. After that trip, her nightmares revolved around saving the world's poor. She wrote later about a new dream. In this one she was the only one alive. "Upon me rested the responsibility of making a wagon wheel."[11] The wheel would revive life. No surprise that her childhood heroes were antislavery activist John Brown, women's voting rights promoter Lucy Stone, and her father's friend Abraham Lincoln.[12]

Jane always seemed a frail child. At about age four she suffered a bout of **Pott's disease**, a form of **tuberculosis** that settles in the spine. The disease left Jane with a deformed spine and severe back pain that would haunt her for her entire life. Her toes pointed inward, and her back grew crooked, tilting her head to one side. Her pale and delicate appearance made her look sickly.

Although no one else believed it, Jane thought of herself as an "ugly duckling." She had her father's wide, piercing eyes and brown hair and looked like a cute little girl. But she was by nature quiet and dreamy and often looked sad. She was sure she wasn't good-looking enough to be seen in her handsome father's presence. She wrote about how she would seek out an uncle to walk with after church, so others wouldn't think this "homely" girl belonged to such a handsome man as her father.[13]

MAJOR FAMILY LIFE CHANGES

In 1868, when Jane turned eight years old, John Addams married Ann Hostetter Haldeman. Ann's first husband, William J. Haldeman, had been a customer at John's Fremont bank. Sadly, the man had died the year before. Ann's presence gave Mary a chance to move on with her life. She returned to school instead of having to care for her sickly sister and a large home. Even with a governess to assist her, Mary had found the job overwhelming.

Jane's new stepmother was strong-willed. Around town Ann had a reputation for being stuck-up and quick to anger. Some said her first husband had spoiled her by giving her anything she wanted. Rumors spread that she always got her way. At her new home, she refused to give in to her spoiled stepchild as others had. Some suggested that, early on, Ann was a bossy and clingy mother, and she and Jane clashed often.

Still, Ann understood children who had lost a parent at an early age. Her own mother had died when she was young. Ann immediately made Jane and her brother and sisters feel comfortable and safe. She went out of her way to be generous and motherly. Ann was also a

Ann Hostetter Haldeman, Jane's stepmother, and John Addams in their wedding photo.

Courtesy of the Swarthmore College Peace Collection

talented musician and avid reader. Many evenings, she played guitar and sang, often directing the children in plays.

When Jane left The Homestead for good to open Hull-House, Ann took in a nine-year-old neighbor girl, Mary Fry, to help her family after the death of her mother. Perhaps Ann just needed someone to need her.

Ann came with a bonus: two sons. Henry, sometimes called Harry, was eighteen, about the same age as Alice. Later, Henry and Alice married—to their parents' disapproval. It was not clear what the problem was, although maybe the parents saw an unhappy marriage ahead. George was six months younger than Jane, who was age seven at the time her father remarried. George and Jane became fast friends. Jane wrote in her diary about how they painted pictures and played word games, croquet, and chess together. During evenings, they played charades, Old Maid, and hopscotch. Jane and George studied Latin and history in the same class at Cedarville Elementary.

Jane's favorite times, however, were when the two explored the Norway pine woods and played endless outdoor games. "We had of course our favorite places and trees and birds and flowers. It is hard to reproduce the companionship which children establish with

Cedarville School class photo with Jane (second from left with her head off to the side) and George (second from right, bottom row).

Courtesy of the Cedarville Area Historical Society

nature. . . . We brought all the snakes we [found] during our excursions."[14] They liked watching them slither and slide. Jane expanded her love of nature with George and their explorations.

The Addams siblings stayed close through writing letters, many of which commented on Jane and George. In August 1871 Mary wrote Alice that "Jennie and George never seem to be quite as contented as when they are alone, without any company."[15] During the years since George had arrived at The Homestead, he had helped boost Jane's spirits. She was becoming a more confident and cheerful teen.

Did You Know?

In the mid-1800s, many girls named Jane used the nickname *Jennie.* The name came from Jenny Lind, an internationally popular Swedish opera singer at the time. The Addams family preferred *Jennie* until Jane graduated from Cedarville School. As a sign of her growing independence from home, she dropped both her first name, *Laura,* and her nickname, *Jennie,* when she left for higher learning. She preferred the name *Jane* instead.

Jane wrote a lot about the influence of her father and his emphasis on fairness. But she rarely touched on other child-hood experiences that accounted for much of her thinking and actions. Three threads ran through her early years that most likely affected her evolving philosophy of life. They were death, illness, and a love of nature.

Losing a mother so young, even if cared for by a loving older sister, has lasting effects on any child. As a youngster, Jane knew that three of her siblings had died within their first couple years of life. Her sister Martha died at age sixteen. The crowning loss was yet to come—her father—when Jane was twenty-one and questioning what to do with her life.

From a young age, Jane was considered physically weak and was often in considerable pain. Yet there is little or no mention of her ever complaining about her health. No one knows the difference that constant pain made in her thinking.

Between the deaths of others and her own illness, Jane learned through experience that nothing in life is certain or permanent. Anything important needed to get done immediately.

Nature and the outdoors were the most positive con-stants in her life. Jane loved wandering her family's estate. She adored her time with George exploring the outdoors. They continued their walks later at Rockford Female **Sem-inary.** Her early focus at Hull House was on children and how they needed space, clean air, and time to explore their environments. Jane started the system of playgrounds in Chi-cago and arranged for campgrounds to get city children into nature to explore.

THREE

ROADMAP FOR THE FUTURE
Troublemaker

So much of our time is spent in preparation, so much in routine, and so much in sleep, we find it difficult to have any experience at all.

—Jane Addams

Jane's stepmother, Ann, once hired a **phrenologist** to examine Jane. This questionable type of doctor measured Jane's skull and its bumps to predict mental traits, an unproven but popular science at the time. The doctor pronounced the almost-sixteen-year-old as having "rather an evenness of temperament but . . . strength of feeling and energy. . . . If she thinks a thing is true, she thinks it with all her might. . . . Strong will and inclined to be very obstinate." He further recommended that Jane should turn her talents to drawing and music.[1]

But Jane had other ideas. Her main passion was history, drawn from all the books she had read in her father's library. And she liked biology, in part due to George's influence. With an eye toward science, she had hoped to take advanced studies at Smith College. This institution in Northampton, Massachusetts, opened in 1871 as one of the first places of higher learning for young women. Jane so wanted to go there that she traveled to Northampton and passed the college entrance exams.

Her father, however, never thought much of educating girls and women beyond the basics needed to be good community helpers and wives. This ran counter to his belief in education for all. With his nineteenth-century thinking, however, he preferred to keep his daughters closer to home for school. John also served on the board at Rockford Female Seminary in Rockford, Illinois, where Jane's two elder sisters had received their advanced education. He wanted Jane to go there too.

Jane found Rockford Seminary lacking. Classes covered only a limited range of topics. Even though the state had awarded it college status, the school issued only diplomas rather than professional degrees. Jane wanted a formal degree.

With great disappointment, Jane packed her bags for Rockford Female Seminary in fall 1877. She traveled by carriage about thirty-three miles to the school overlooking the Rock River. There she met

Nature surrounded the early Rockford Seminary.
Wikimedia Commons

Principal Anna P. Sill. Starting in 1849, Miss Sill ran the seminary with an iron fist for thirty years. All religions were welcome, but Miss Sill viewed it as her job to turn out **missionaries**, women who would travel to remote areas to promote Christianity and provide services, such as education, social service, and healthcare. Miss Sill considered future wives "home missionaries."[2]

Miss Sill expected students to follow a rigid daily program to reinforce their future role of self-sacrifice. During the week, Jane ate plain, often tasteless food with applesauce at every dinner. Each Sunday featured cold meat, baked potatoes, and baked beans. Miss Sill even directed students to bring their own eating utensils. On top of this, she required regular fasting days without any food at all.[3]

Unlike at home, Jane tended a woodstove to keep herself warm in her single, bare bedroom. She cleaned her own room and washed and changed her own bed linens. Usually, the family governess or maid performed these duties for her at The Homestead. Miss Sill required students to dress in drab clothes and never to curl their hair. The message was that a simple, clean, and orderly environment equaled a clean and orderly mind. Students and their poorly paid teachers essentially lived like the missionaries they were expected to become.

Miss Sill programmed every part of the day. Each student kept a list of rules and the things they had done wrong. List inspection occurred monthly. "The emphasis of the whole routine was on study and religious discipline—Miss Sill's religion," wrote James Weber Linn, Jane's nephew and biographer.[4] Besides classes in Latin, **rhetoric** (the study of effective language), **physiology** (the study of the body and its functions), history, and geography, which changed slightly from year to year, there was constant Bible study. Church and silent prayer took place every Sunday. Miss Sill banned all waltzing, card playing, and theater.[5]

Miss Sill also required specific exercise. No matter the weather, students walked a circular wooden path for an hour. Jane often paced around the outdoor walkway up to thirty times. Miss Sill and her frustrating rules must have sucked the fun out of walks and every other activity. Still, Jane thought these walks better than the regular Saturday morning horseback rides that her stepmother had demanded, even knowing how much back pain they caused Jane.

One bright spot for Jane was meeting Ellen Gates Starr at the seminary. The two became close friends. Jane loved how Ellen's poetry and her articles on art in the school magazine showed wit and intelligence. The two continued writing to each other after Ellen left school, and they visited together at Jane's Cedarville home often.

Success at Rockford Female Seminary helped Jane gain new confidence in her looks and abilities. She was a petite five feet, three inches tall and weighed ninety-five pounds. Her head now tilted less, and her pulled-back brown hair framed a delicate face with large light eyes. Once she had grown comfortable at school, she radiated friendly confidence. Classmates were immediately drawn to her curious intelligence and willingness to engage with them. As one classmate wrote, "We never [questioned] . . . why we liked to go to her room so that it was always crowded when the sacred 'engaged' sign was not hung out. We just knew . . . that however mopey it might be elsewhere there was intellectual ozone [pure air] in her vicinity."[6]

Many late nights, Jane gathered her friends together and covered the door window to prevent light from peeking out the doorway. They munched on popcorn and cooked oysters sent from home on the wood stove. Often, they read to each other or discussed books they had read.

Jane clashed with Miss Sill almost from the beginning. "She does everything from love of God *alone*, and I do not like that," Jane wrote in her diary.[7] She agreed that everyone should be useful, as Miss Sill urged, but Jane wanted to define what *she* thought useful. Like Jane, Miss Sill was smart, passionate, and always right. But Jane refused to blindly accept all that this woman required, and she often attempted small rebellions.

On one occasion, Jane and four friends wanted to experience what British author Thomas De Quincey wrote in his book *Dreams*.

So they drugged themselves with **opium** powder, which back then was thought a safe drug to cure nervous disorders. Within minutes, the girls felt disoriented. Trying to stay out of trouble with Miss Sill, they talked instead to a friendly teacher. She told them firmly to rest in their separate rooms. But the teacher also made it clear that they must appear for family worship—no matter what their condition. They did, and they vowed never to try anything like that again.

The girls were often urged to confess their sins and, of course, to show interest in religion. But Jane never followed a specific religion and refused to confess any sins. Teachers constantly approached Jane to ask her to give herself over to religion and future missionary work. They visited her at quiet times to try and convince her to change her nonreligious ways. But Jane's guide was her father's moral training. Like him, she never committed to a particular religion.

Friends looked to Jane for leadership. If a dispute occurred with Miss Sill, they preferred that Jane deal with her. They even believed Jane's word over that of the school principal. On one occasion, Miss Sill mispronounced the name *Don Quixote* during a lesson. When Jane corrected her, the other students followed her lead and chuckled. Miss Sill was so furious at being corrected—and laughed at *afterward*—that she suspended class for two days. Jane was angry about the unfair punishment, especially because she believed she was correct. She was so upset that she grabbed a friend's hymn book in chapel and wrote, "Life's a burden, beat it. Life's a duty, dare it. Life's a thorn crown, wear it. And spurn to be a coward."[8]

Despite her strong nature, Jane followed most of the rigid rules and applied herself to her studies. She worked hard to catch up in subjects that had not been taught in her hometown country school. Her grades always topped everyone else's.

Early on, Jane took an interest in writing. She started writing articles for the *Rockford Seminary Magazine,* the school publication. During her second year, she edited the Home Department section of the magazine, adding jokes and lively stories. By her senior year, as editor in chief,

Jane's 1881 class photo at Rockford Seminary. Jane held an umbrella and, like always, never smiled.

Courtesy of Rockford University

Jane changed the tone of the magazine. Her articles featured issues of critical thinking rather than the religious topics that Miss Sill covered. Jane's articles, such as "The Element of Hopefulness in Human Nature," tended to be positive. As editor in chief, she added different issues and created a magazine that turned a profit for the first time.

At the same time Jane entered Rockford Seminary, George moved into a Beloit College dormitory about twenty miles away. Rockford was Beloit's sister school, which meant the two schools often held social and intellectual gatherings together. Jane and her classmates went to class and studied from Monday morning to Friday evening. But on weekends they often took breaks with Beloit College boys. Always properly chaperoned, students went on hayrides, took long walks, and debated.

By fifteen years of age, George was in the boys' college near Jane's school.

Courtesy of the Swarthmore College Peace Collection

Jane loved the opportunity to see George. Since he was studying natural science, she started to consider studying medicine herself. Reports tell of how Jane and a classmate studied **taxidermy**, the art of preserving an animal body by stuffing it. She believed the subject would help her with classes in medicine.

Most Beloit boys studied to be ministers. They often came to Rockford Seminary looking for future brides to accompany them on religious travels. Accounts indicate that another Beloit student, Rollin Salisbury, took an interest in Jane. By then he was president of his class, just as Jane was president of hers. Some whispered that Salisbury proposed marriage to Jane and that she refused him. Years later, despite becoming a geography professor at the nearby University of Chicago, he never visited Hull-House. He remained a bachelor the rest of his life.

Meanwhile, someone closer to Jane expressed romantic interest. George was not a blood relative, so he thought they could marry legally, just as Jane's sister Alice had already married George's older brother, Henry. For some reason, her parents believed that this union, unlike that of Alice and Henry, was a good idea. Jane thought of George as a brother, however, not as a romantic partner. Her decision not to accept his proposal of marriage strained relations with her stepmother that never healed.

Although Rockford Female Seminary had gained state permission to award college degrees in 1847, it had never done so. Instead, it awarded only diplomas. Jane was on a constant quest for the seminary to take its rightful position as a formal college that offered the

ROCKFORD COLLEGE · Rockford, Illinois

Name **Addams, Laura Jane**   ENTERED **September 1877**   SEX **F**
ADDRESS OF STUDENT   DATE AND PLACE OF BIRTH

NAME & ADDRESS OF PARENT, GUARDIAN OR SPOUSE   DEGREE **September 6, 1860   Cedarville, Illinois**
John Huy & Anna Holderman Addams   DATE
Cedarville, Illinois   MAJOR FIELD **B. A.**   **June 1881**
                                                                                             TOTAL

                                                             5 HRS.   GD PTS

ADMISSION UNITS					ACCEPTED FROM
English	Gen. Math	Gen. Sci.	Soc. Stud.	Misc. Subj.	
Spanish	Alg.	Chem.	U.S. Hist.	TOTAL	**Cedarville School**
French	Geom.	Physics	World Hist.	DEFICIENCIES	
German	Trig.		Civics		
Latin	Coll. Alg.				
					RANK

COURSE NO.	TITLE	GD.	S.H.	COURSE NO	TITLE	GD	S.H
	1st Series 1877-78				**1st Series 1879-80**		
Latin	Virgil, Caesar	9.0			Greek	9.7	
Nat. Sci.	Physiology	9.7			Cicero	9.9	
German	German	10.0		Hist.& Lit	Eng.Lit,Milt.,Spencer,Young	10.0	
	Music	9.0			German	9.7	
	Bible History	9.8			Astronomy	9.8	
Hist.& Lit.	Rhet. Comp.	8.5			Bible	9.7	
	2nd Series 1877-78				**2nd Series 1879-80**		
Hist.& Lit.	Rhetoric - Comp.	9.5			Med. History	9.9	
	Music	9.8		Hist.& Lit	Rhet. Crit.Read.(Milton)Comp.	9.9	
Latin	Caesar, Virgil	9.0			Solid Geometry	9.8	
Nat. Sci.	Botany	9.0			Horace	9.6	
Math.	University Algebra	10.0			Greek	9.6	
	German	9.6			German	10.0	
	Bible History	8.5			Bible	9.9	
	1st Series 1878-79				**1st Series 1880-81**		
Math.	Geometry, Plane	9.8			Mental Philosophy	9.8	
	German	9.9			Evidences of Christianity	9.7	
	Greek	9.7			German	10.0	
	Ancient History	9.8			Chemistry	9.9	
	Outline	9.8			Bible	9.8	
	Civil Government	9.7					
Hist.& Lit.	Crit. Rdg. Shksp.,Macaulay	9.8			**2nd Series 1880-81**		
					Geology - Mineralogy	10.0	
	2nd Series 1878-79				German	10.0	
	Trigonometry	9.9			Spherical Trigonometry	9.9	
	German	10.0			Crit.Rdg.Anc't.Lit. Comp.	9.5	
	American Literature	9.7			Latin (Tacitus)	9.9	
	Modern History	9.8			Moral Philosophy	9.9	
	Greek	9.5			Bible	9.9	
	Reading (Shakespeare)	9.9					
					Four Year Average		
					Scholarship: 9.862		
					Department : 10.0		
					Average : 9.931		

Rockford College
ARCHIVES

Transcripts of Jane Addams from Rockford Female Seminary, 1881. Jane was her class valedictorian, receiving the highest grades in her class with a 9.86 grade point average out of 10 possible points.

Courtesy of Rockford University

same degrees that male institutions awarded. She and another student pushed to take advanced courses in mathematics in the hope that such learning would help persuade state officials that women were as intelligent as men. Some teachers at Rockford Female Seminary were active in trying to secure the woman's vote. Showing that women could handle the same coursework as men might convince state lawmakers that women could handle the same right to vote as well.

To this end, the students applied to allow Rockford Female Seminary to participate in a statewide college debate. The seminary became the first state women's school to receive that honor. To her surprise, Jane was selected to represent the school. When she went to the event, however, she discovered that she was the only woman. For Jane, it meant that she was representing all college women. Jane came in fifth place, a solid middle spot. But she scored a victory for what she called the "Woman's Cause."[9]

Back at the seminary, Jane persevered to add more difficult courses. By graduation in 1882 she had earned the title of **valedictorian**, top in her class. For her efforts, Jane asked for a degree but received only a diploma. Still, she never gave up. One year after graduation, Jane returned to Rockford Female Seminary to accept the school's first degree, becoming the school's first official college graduate. Jane later would receive fourteen honorary degrees. None meant as much to her as the degree from Rockford Female Seminary. Whatever the future held, the degree marked a high point in her young life.

Did You Know?

John Addams required his daughters to learn bread baking. When they reached age twelve, he ordered each daughter, including Jane, to present him with a pleasing bread. One reason was to learn at least one household activity. His focus on bread baking also probably reflected the fact that he owned the town grain mill.[10]

FOUR

FALSE STARTS

The highest moralists have taught that without the advance and improvement of the whole, no man [or woman] can hope for the lasting improvement of his [or her] . . . individual condition.

—Jane Addams

By the end of her time at Rockford Female Seminary, Jane had decided to pursue "the study of medicine and live with the poor."[1] She agreed with her father that women should have resources equal to those available to men. To that end, she believed that science was the best course to prove women's equality. Surely if more women excelled in the sciences, state and federal legislatures would have to take women seriously enough to allow them to vote. She offered this connection to her father in the hopes that he would agree to her attending medical school.

Hoping to enter medical school, Jane filled vacations with study of earthworms, rocks, and pressed plants. Her spirits lifted at the thought of fulfilling her dream to help others through medicine. But in the summer before she left for medical college, disaster struck.

Twenty-one-year-old Jane, George, and their parents rode a horse-drawn carriage to northern Wisconsin where John Addams wanted to inspect copper mills as an investment for his bank. While there, John's **appendix** burst, and he died within thirty-six hours. His death crushed Jane. She wrote to Ellen Starr, "The greatest sorrow that can ever come to me had passed, and I hope it is only a question of time until I get my moral purposes straightened."[2]

Jane forced herself to carry on. But her father's death proved a severe blow that quietly took its toll. More than ever, she was determined to study medicine and longed to leave home. In his will, Jane's father left her a sizable amount of money. Two-thirds had gone to her stepmother, and the rest was split among his children. He was a very rich man when he died. Jane inherited enough to provide her with a sense of freedom and the power to make her own decisions.

In winter 1881 Jane left for the Woman's Medical College of Philadelphia, where she passed early exams. But she lasted only until spring. Her childhood Pott's disease flared up again. Pain forced her into bedrest for the next six months at her sister Alice's home in Mitchellville, Iowa. During that time, while reading and resting, Jane realized that pursuing medicine no longer interested her. George was the real scientist of the two of them.

Jane thought that there must be other ways to serve the less fortunate. But which road was for her? Jane was relieved when the doctor forbade her to return to the university clinic and classes. Illness—and probably her father's death—had triggered mental as well as physical exhaustion. **Depression** set in. She felt like a failure. For the next few years, Jane struggled to find her sense of purpose. During part of that time, she stayed with her married sisters before going back to Cedarville.

After Jane returned to Cedarville, her severe pain recurred. She spent another six months at Alice's home. Alice's husband—now Doctor Henry Haldeman—operated on Jane's spine. Afterward, he fitted her with a whalebone binder to help keep her back straight, but it dug into her back and chest. Still, she wore the tight wrap for another year. Although sore from the binder, Jane admitted that the back pain had lessened, and she walked straighter.

Twenty-one-year-old Jane found her stepmother oppressive and pushed to leave home.

Throughout these years of uncertainty, Jane wrote in her journals. Her comments swung between hope for her future and despair at what she might do. She desperately looked for direction. After her surgery, Dr. Haldeman advised her to travel overseas and calm her nerves. At that time many women with money, including Jane's two older sisters, toured Europe and other places after graduation. In 1883 Jane, her stepmother, and six friends boarded a ship in Philadelphia for a twenty-day journey to Ireland. During her travels, Jane continued writing in her journal. But she wrote little about the usual tourist attractions. Instead, she detailed the lives of the everyday people she found in different neighborhoods. At each stop, she asked about wages, jobs, and homes, and if families found enough to eat.

Over the next two years, Jane discovered what she thought of as her real education—seeing how others lived beyond Cedarville and Rockford. From Ireland the party traveled through England to Holland and on to Germany, Austria, Italy, Greece, Switzerland, and France. What Jane remembered most, however, were the miserable conditions in parts of London with its filthy, narrow streets and alleyways. The images that stayed with her involved children begging for food. She couldn't get the hungry faces or the arms reaching out for unfit food out of her mind.

Jane remained restless throughout the group's travels. She knew that she was lucky to be part of the first group of women to receive advanced education and culture beyond skills for the home. But for what purpose? She wanted to use her education for greater good. "I gradually reached the conviction that the first generation of college women had developed too exclusively the power of *acquiring* knowledge. . . . Somewhere in the process of 'being educated' they had lost that . . . healthful reaction resulting in *activity*."[3]

An older Ann Addams at her writing desk.

Courtesy of the Swarthmore College Peace Collection

Toward the end of their travels, a message came that Jane's sister Mary, who was pregnant with her fifth child, was very sick. After twenty-one months away, the women returned home immediately. Jane rushed to assist her frail sister and tend her many children. She stayed, on and off, for the next two years in the Illinois towns of Harvard and Genesco. Jane's role as caretaker had begun. In a letter to Ellen, she confirmed the importance of nature for children: "If you don't take little children out in the yard to spend the morning you simply can't see their unbounded delight and extravagant joy when they see a bird taking his bath."[4]

Once back in Cedarville, Ann Addams decided that she and her stepdaughter would winter in Baltimore, Maryland. It was 1885, and George was studying for an advanced medical degree at Johns Hopkins University. Ann schemed about pushing Jane into a wider social life. She also hoped to nurture a more romantic relationship between

Jane and George. Ann wanted them married. But Jane hated small talk and never liked the card parties or other social events her stepmother preferred. Jane knew that one day important work would come to her. That concern outweighed the idea of marriage and fancy gatherings. Jane understood that women's limited options at the time meant marriage *or* a career—never both.

Ann's other scheme failed, too. Jane had always liked George, but her nearness to him during this time didn't change her lack of interest in a romance with him. George responded by becoming distant and sullen. These conditions only worsened as he aged. Jane's niece Marcet remembers that Jane's repeated rejection of George came during his time of intense, advanced studies. "He was so torn within himself and . . . so indifferent to life that he neglected . . . his work. Brain and body collapsed and, after an acute illness, . . . he spent his remaining years as a semi-invalid and recluse in the Cedarville Homestead."[5]

While in Baltimore, Jane searched for a meaningful way to fill her time. Several days a week, she volunteered at a home for older Black women. That experience led to visits to an orphanage that trained girls for work, mostly as servants—one of the few job options for young women of color at that time. Both ventures made Jane feel alive with the value of giving. Ellen Starr later told a reporter that Jane had discovered in Baltimore that "after a lecture or a social evening she would feel quite exhausted . . . but after a morning . . . in the Johns Hopkins Home, she was actually physically better than if she had stayed in bed."[6]

Jane spent a couple winters in Baltimore with Ann. She returned to Cedarville for summers. During the second summer, she investigated how Alice's husband cared for family investments, including hers. Henry Haldeman had stopped practicing medicine and now worked at the Girard, Kansas, extension of the bank once owned by her father. Jane saw firsthand her stepbrother's sloppy investing. Thereafter, Jane was determined to manage her own accounts.

Letters from Ellen told of visits to European historical places. She was researching artworks and artists to share with her Chicago public school students. Jane desperately needed a break from helping her two sisters with their growing families, so she decided to join Ellen. Jane encouraged another friend from Rockford Seminary, Sarah Anderson, to come along. They set sail from Hoboken, New Jersey, on December 14, 1887, this time without Jane's stepmother. Illness haunted Jane, both on the ship and after they reached Europe. She worried that she had overestimated her own health and strength. Jane stayed in Ireland but urged Ellen and Sarah to visit other countries without her.

Once healthier, Jane joined her friends in Madrid, Spain. While there, a visit to a bullfight jolted Jane into a new way of thinking. Everyone else in their party of six had left the bullfight in horror. Jane found herself unfazed, even after seeing bullfighters tossed about, as well as dead horses and bulls. Her friends were shocked that she had stayed so long watching the bloodshed. Not until later did the significance of the event hit Jane. She worried she had become numb from her idleness. Jane knew she could no longer deceive herself into thinking that she was seeking some truth that would magically appear. She determined to act on a plan, one that she had envisioned long ago. She would live among the poor.

The first step toward carrying out her plan was to present her vision to her good friend Ellen. Jane worried that Ellen would think her idea silly. Instead, Ellen jumped at the chance to partner in the new project. While Ellen left to finish her art research in Italy, Jane headed to London's East End to meet with volunteers at Toynbee Hall, the first successful university-connected settlement house. Jane now had a plan and someone to work with her. She sailed home with a new vision for her future. Now she had to figure out how and where to execute it.

British settlement workers believed that they could better assist the working poor by incorporating community values into their programs. They took a parental, sometimes religious, approach to do-gooding. University of Oxford graduate Edward Denison opened the first British settlement in the poor Stepney neighborhood in 1867. Denison was a bishop's son who taught children and advocated for better local housing. Within two years, however, he was forced to scrap the program due to his ill health. He died a year later.

Another privileged Oxford graduate, Arnold Toynbee, moved into the working-class Whitechapel area of East London in 1875. He also created an education center. His focus, however, was on offering lectures on politics and the economy, things that were probably not most important in the lives of nearby poor, uneducated workers. Another drawback was the fact that Toynbee acted superior to his neighbors. He talked about his "delicate emotions" while facing "the great mass of filthy misery."[7]

Toynbee's work was cut short, too, as he died at age thirty-two. But these early efforts caught the attention of the London press. Followers of Toynbee reopened the center again for university students to continue what he had begun. They called the residence Toynbee Hall. Jane's visit to Toynbee Hall formed the basis for her future Hull-House and for other settlement houses in Great Britain and the United States.

Did You Know?

Jane received her diploma from Rockford Seminary with the name Laura Jane Addams. A year later she returned to accept the college's first formal degree. This one read "Jane Addams." The name change signaled her independence from her family and past.

FIVE

HEAD RABBLE-ROUSER

> Let us say again that the lessons of great men [and
> women] are lost unless they re-enforce . . . the
> highest demands which we make upon ourselves.
>
> —Jane Addams

Once an idea took hold, Jane devoted herself to making a plan of action. She put her finances in order in 1889 and joined Ellen in Chicago, where together they founded Hull-House. They hired a young housekeeper, Mary Keyser, to take care of everyday chores. Still, Jane and Ellen willingly handled every aspect of running Hull-House, including housekeeping.

After its renovation, Hull-House opened to the curious—and the suspicious. Neighbors wondered what these two well-dressed but strange women were doing in their neighborhood. What did they want from them? Why were they opening their home to strangers? What the curious found was a welcoming place. "Slender, sunny-haired, quick-moving" Jane personally welcomed everyone who came through the door.[1]

Neighbors soon discovered that Jane and Ellen merely wanted to know what *they* needed so that Hull-House could provide it for them. Neighbors described the kinds of activities that would help improve their lives. They needed information about job and housing opportunities and a place to gather and socialize. Jane and Ellen gradually added cultural programs, activities, and informational classes to benefit their neighbors. Grateful immigrants and others came to share a meal, have tea, or attend a dance, social, or performance. Some neighbors arrived at Hull-House to escape violence at home and then stayed on.

Word spread that Hull-House was also open to people who wanted to learn how to improve social services. Some who visited were university educators hoping to conduct research into health and neighborhood improvement. Many came to live, sort of like at boarding school. Others arrived to arrange particular activities or events. Classes filled with volunteer instructors. Slowly, the number of volunteers grew.

By the end of the first year, Hull-House had received fifty thousand people. These included neighbors attending events and classes, volunteers who helped provide services and teach classes, wealthy

Reception and other areas of Hull-House open to guests of all ages.
Courtesy of Rockford University

Days began early at Hull-House. By 7:30 a.m. volunteer bakers filled the air with smells of coffee and breads. Teachers, clerks, and factory inspectors stopped for freshly prepared food to nourish their day. They passed the paper carrier who slipped a range of newspapers safely under the door-mat. About twenty-five parents dropped off young children for day care on their way to work.

After the first rush of people, another wave arrived to check job opportunities. Hull-House opened a branch of the Chicago Relief and Aid Society to help folks find jobs and assistance. At nine o'clock, a visiting nurse arrived to pack her bags before making her rounds. The nurse visited families in need of food and medical attention as well as police stations to look for a lost boy or girl.

Cooks, many of them volunteers, served lunch in the house dining room. Afterward, kindergarten students played and learned skills in the Children's Building. Classes in the gym and the children's chorus and band filled the halls with music and laughter. After school, older immigrant children studied English, their new language. Others brushed up on ancient Greek in the hopes of entering college. Nearby, the Woman's Club met.

Dinner at six o'clock gathered residents and guests in the dining room. Jane presided at one end of the largest table, and Ellen sat at the other end. This was the time for lively discussion, debate, and coming together. Diners lingered—at least until evening activities began.

After dinner, older children and adults attended a range of classes from grammar to needlework to higher math. Livelier visitors joined dance and drama clubs. Others preferred games and sports in the gym building. Once a month, lectures or casual talks took place. Every subject and opinion was welcome.

These activities took place in addition to much more at Hull-House. Guests could borrow pictures and books, view art exhibits, browse the library, and join holiday festivities and regular Sunday lectures and concerts. Jane remained committed to the healing qualities of nature. She expanded the outdoor playground and provided getaways for children at summer camps. All these programs offered safe places for anyone who needed one.[2]

donors, and the simply curious. Counts from the second year averaged two thousand visitors a week. Mary Keyser kept records of donations and visitor numbers. These records marked the beginning of modern social studies and research.[3] Over time, the settlement would change life not only for the neighbors of Hull-House but also for the city of Chicago.

PROGRAMS

Jane and her growing staff created a social and cultural center. At this settlement, all ages and nationalities could find something of interest to enrich their lives. At first Jane introduced activities that she had enjoyed growing up. For example, she organized a lending library, as her father had created in Cedarville. Two weeks after opening, Jane and Ellen invited young women to an evening reading party, where the guests shared what kinds of programs they would prefer. Visitors learned quickly that Hull-House embraced their participation and ideas.

Many of the initial programs focused on children. At first the drawing room housed the kindergarten, a relatively new idea in early education. The kindergarten gained such popularity that child services expanded to include a day nursery and infant care center. These safe places for children eased the burdens of working and overwhelmed mothers.

"The day nursery was housed in a wooden building around the corner," wrote Jane's niece Marcet, who visited each summer with her mother, Alice. "When mothers brought their children, they were tubbed and changed into clean clothes. . . . But it was disturbing to me to see them changed, at night, back into their own garments, which were too often ragged and dirty." After Marcet visited some homes with older siblings, she found "crowded, noisy, ill-smelling tenements." She then "began to have a faint glimmer . . . of what Aunt Jane was trying to do."[4]

Always looking to improve the area, Jane called out the owner of some nearby decaying houses and stables to fix his properties. Rather than paying to improve his buildings, the owner agreed to donate them to Hull-House. Jane tore down the buildings and used the land for a public playground, the first in the city. The former owner of the land even bought equipment and paid the property taxes. Later, the playground came under the care of the new City Playground Commission and led to the creation of many more public playgrounds in Chicago.

A cornerstone of Hull-House was the belief that discussion and shared activities among diverse people led to understanding. With immigrants visiting Hull-House from so many cultures, Jane created activities such as dances, meals, and holiday gatherings to celebrate these cultures. Learning English allowed immigrants to communicate with each other and to improve their standing at their jobs. The settlement taught other practical educational classes at the secondary and college levels and hosted workshops and clubs in homemaking skills.

As donations increased, Hull-House expanded with separate buildings for a theater, gym, swimming pool, and employment office. With time, Jane noticed the need for separate resident buildings for men and women. "Children came to play; the young to act or draw or dance; girls in trouble who had been turned out of their homes; men out of work or on the run; the sick and the tired and the frightened and the lonely, and along with them scholars from universities [who came to study, live, or volunteer at Hull-House]."[5]

Children enjoyed a range of activities, including art class.
National Archives

At first, Jane funded Hull-House with the money she had inherited from her father: $50,000, which equals $1.6 million today.[6] Although the amount was sizable, she realized that the settlement could not secure a lasting future without other, more stable income. As more people learned about Hull-House and its programs, many of the volunteers donated money as well as time. They saw merit in what Jane and others were trying to do. For some wealthy donors, supporting a settlement reduced their feelings of guilt for having so much. As Jane wrote, "Hull-House had become fashionable."[7]

Jane knew that her father would have approved of Hull-House. Therefore, she assumed that her stepmother, who had inherited two-thirds of his estate, would help support Hull-House as he would have. But Ann still resented Jane's rejection of George. She never donated or visited. Jane found her so ungenerous that when visiting Cedarville, she stayed instead with her brother Weber, who now owned the old Addams mill and a nearby home.[8]

Jane spent considerable time searching for other sources of income. Soon after opening Hull-House, help arrived. One of the first nonresident volunteers was Mary Rozet Smith, a former art student of Ellen's. When her friend Jenny Dow volunteered as the first Hull-House kindergarten teacher, twenty-year-old Mary tagged along. She never left. About a month after the settlement opened, Mary began working with rowdy immigrant boys to keep them off the streets. She bought chess sets and pool tables to engage them. Best of all, she thrilled the boys by reading stories. One biographer wrote: "They listened with enchanted attention. Their young imaginations took wing: each boy could feel himself capable of great things. They chose to call their group Young Heroes Club."[9]

Besides the boys' club, Mary founded the Hull-House Music School. She donated a theater organ and helped with drama productions. Five years after arriving, she was elected to the board that directed the management of Hull-House.

Mary Rozet Smith and Jane Addams clicked at first meeting.
Swarthmore College Peace Collection

Finding money was a constant concern for Jane. Within a short time after arriving at Hull-House, Mary took over much of that job. Still, Jane spent many hours speaking to social and business groups to interest them in Hull-House. She penned articles about Hull-House and about her beliefs in peace and helping the poor. These writings appeared in dozens of national magazines. Jane wrote books that expanded her following and drew attention to Hull-House. These activities provided a small but steady income to expand Hull-House and its activities.

The first new building held the Butler Gallery. This addition boasted an art exhibition hall, a reading room, and a studio for art classes, Ellen's passion. Some complained that fine art was not a priority for Hull-House neighbors. But the popular museum lasted from its founding in 1891 until the Hull-House complex was demolished in 1963. Ellen's passion turned into a lending library of art reproductions, decorations in public school classrooms, and a book bindery in addition to art and music schools. The lending library, in turn, blossomed into the first art program for city public schools.

A group of neighborhood women and some volunteers organized at Hull-House and called themselves the Jane Club. The club came about after factory worker protests caused women to lose their homes. In some cases employers locked out their workers who protested. In other situations, workers walked out, or called a **strike**, against unfair conditions on the job. Either case often resulted in women unable to pay their rent. The Jane Club raised money through Hull-House to rent a low-cost boarding house for these out-of-work women. Within the first three years, the original two furnished apartments expanded to six. Up to fifty unemployed women now had a place to live.[10]

Raising money for this project posed a particular conflict for Jane. One contributor offered to donate $20,000 and another offered $50,000. In exchange, they wanted Jane to stop pushing for a new Illinois law to regulate factory pay and conditions. But factory workers already barely survived on the little pay they received. Jane rejected the contributors' offers. The daughter of Honest John Addams could never take bribes.

In 1900 Jane opened the Labor Museum. The museum combined working crafters, classes, exhibits, craft samples, and displays that illustrated stages of development, including bookbinding and metalworking.[11]

One visitor noticed that the Labor Museum served another important purpose. Some children felt superior to their non-English-speaking parents. "For such children the Labor Museum was an eye-opener. When they saw crowds of well-dressed Americans standing around admiring what Italian, Irish, German, and Scandinavian mothers could do, their [scorn] for their mothers often vanished."[12]

When Polish author and activist Hilda Satt visited Hull-House as a young child, Jane Addams greeted her at the door. Jane immediately brought her to the Labor Museum. "I feel that she sensed what I needed most at that time. She turned me over to Miss Mary Hill, who

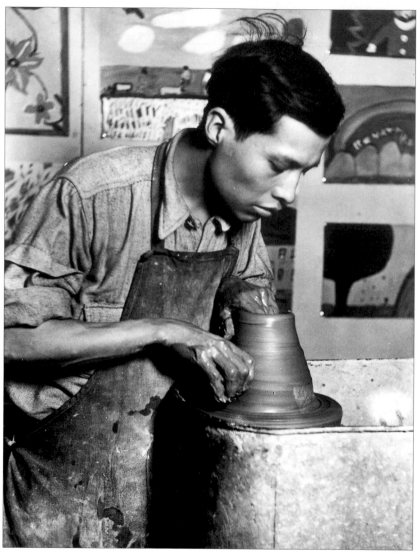

The Labor Museum highlighted skills in pottery, metalwork, weaving, and a range of crafts.

National Archives

had charge of the museum. . . . Our first stop [on my tour] was in front of four cases that . . . showed the evolution of cotton, wool, silk, and linen. I recall how surprised I was when I discovered that cotton grew out of the ground. . . . Miss Hill [then] asked me whether I would like to learn to weave something that was typically American. Yes, I was ready to learn almost anything."[13]

BRANCHING INTO THE NEIGHBORHOOD

Once Jane and other residents identified ills affecting their neighbors, they looked into the causes. After an investigation in 1895, Jane and the Hull-House Women's Club linked open garbage and lack of collection to higher illness and death rates in the Nineteenth Ward where they lived. They found littered alleys and open wooden garbage boxes on sidewalks where children often played. City records showed more than one thousand formal health violations.

Once Jane heard that the city had awarded a contract for garbage removal, she requested pickup around Hull House. "My paper was thrown out, but the incident induced the mayor to appoint me the garbage inspector of the ward," Jane wrote.[14]

Jane encountered trouble from the beginning. **Alderman** John Powers disliked losing the job that Jane took; Powers used these city jobs to bribe voters who needed work. In turn, he demanded that the job seekers vote for him.

Jane's tasks required her to rise at six o'clock in the morning to follow the garbage collectors. Sometimes she followed wagons so overloaded that they dropped smelly garbage back onto the street. Jane thought that the contractor needed additional wagons to do a good job. The contractor insisted that he would lose money by adding wagons. Jane discovered that he had a side business carting away garbage and dead animals from private stables, for a fee of course. This was at the same time that he was being paid by the city.

Another issue concerned immigrants from cities where garbage was usually thrown into the street. They were unaware that garbage caused disease and that there were other places to put it. Over her next three years as garbage inspector, Jane delicately educated neighbors about their civic duty concerning garbage. The death rate dropped the Nineteenth Ward from third to seventh in the city.

Ultimately, the mayor wanted Jane and her complaints gone. He introduced a measure to combine garbage collection with street repair. This job required potential workers to take an exam, but the exam was open only to men. Clearly, he saw Jane as dangerous.

WHEN TALKING STOPS WORKING

By the late 1800s strikes had become key to gaining worker rights. Yet having no paycheck during those strikes created hardships for workers and their families. Hull-House offered food and a safe place to meet. It provided basic necessities when families ran out of money.

Jane professed to be neutral, never taking sides. She encouraged workers and business owners to find common ground. The Pullman Strike of 1894 challenged her thinking. Struggling after a low point in the economy, railroad car manufacturer George Pullman cut the wages he paid to his workers. But he never cut money that went to his financial backers. More unfairly, he owned Pullman, Illinois, a community that he built to house his railroad car builders. Seeing rent as a way to earn more money for his company, he required all workers to live in Pullman or face firing.

Outraged employees stopped work, halting railroad service into and out of the city. As the stoppage continued, streetcar workers from any railroad carrying Pullman cars also stopped working. With time, employee struggles spread to twenty-seven states and included more than two hundred thousand workers. As the strike dragged on, divisions between the two sides widened. Eventually, the federal government sent armed troops to stop the violence. However, they sided with big business against the unarmed workers.

Jane was selected for an Industrial Committee of city leaders to help moderate discussions between the two sides. Ultimately, her considerable efforts to bring both sides together failed. Worse yet, the media accused Addams—and by extension Hull-House—of being proworker and antibusiness. Her neutrality was no longer taken seriously.

Jane lost friends among the middle and upper classes who saw her as a "traitor to her class." She angered workers, too, because she refused to commit to a side. Still, Hull-House remained a safe haven for anyone battling factory and business injustices.

JANE TAKES ON CROOKED POLITICIANS

Garbage collection and union negotiations were Jane's first attempt to change Chicago government. From then on she became a thorn in the sides of politicians at all levels, particularly Alderman Powers. At first he appeared to work with Jane, helping in matters like garbage collection and donating turkeys to Hull-House at Christmas. He soon tired of her meddling.

In 1898 Jane and her residents expanded research into the decaying Taylor Street School, which overflowed with students. She proposed adding another school in the ward. But immigrant men rarely voted, and women could not vote by law. So Powers convinced the Catholic Church to build a Catholic school instead. Jane wanted a free, public school for every child, no matter their religion.

Jane wasn't finished with Powers. She urged men who came to Hull-House to run against him. Not much came of these efforts, except that Powers began attacking Jane in the media. Powers told reporters, "The trouble with Miss Addams is that she is jealous of my charitable work in the ward. Hull-House will be driven from the ward."[15]

That never happened, so Powers started a letter-writing campaign against Jane. One of his supporters emphasized how Jane sought the "defeat of that good, noble, and charitable man John Powers."[16] Jane knew that this "good" man would do anything for a vote. He took bribes, traded bribes with voters, sprang criminals from jail, and lied often. Jane remained determined. She was just beginning to make waves, some that would ripple around the world.

Mary Rozet Smith (1868–1934) lived in Chicago's wealthy Gold Coast neighborhood in a large mansion. Her father had grown rich from owning a successful paper company. Her upbringing included the best private schools and training in teaching and the arts. At times, Mary traveled in Europe with her parents, who groomed her for a life of privilege.

But like Jane, Mary wanted more than tea parties and balls. At age twenty, the tall, fair woman with soft brown curls and kind eyes seemed shy but eager to find meaningful work. She found that work at Hull-House. She invested time and money in Hull-House for the next forty-three years.

Almost from the beginning, Jane felt a special bond with Mary. Within a year, their friendship deepened. Mary became Jane's major financial and emotional support, convincing her father to help fund Hull-House projects. After her father's death, Mary donated money from personal accounts left to her by her parents. Equally important, she opened her home to Jane, so the exhausted woman could rest when Hull-House activities overwhelmed her. Mary and Jane traveled together. Mary monitored Jane's health when old ailments resurfaced or new ones appeared. Many claimed that Jane could not have gotten as much done without Mary's support.[17]

Toward the end of their lives, the two women bought a cottage near Bar Harbor, Maine. The home provided an escape from the constant stresses of Jane's work. Mary never minded supplying most of the funds while staying in Jane's shadow. The two remained close until Mary died in 1934.[18] There has been much speculation about the exact nature of their relationship. Was it romantic or were they good friends? No one will ever know for sure. Before she died, Jane destroyed many of the more personal letters the two women had exchanged.

Did You Know?

Boarders, or residents, paid for room and board and were voted in by other residents in order to stay. Residents met weekly to decide household issues, such as food, housekeeping, and new projects. During the seventy years of Hull-House, residents broke ground in sociology, social work, the arts, and labor issues.

SIX

MORE GOOD TROUBLE

If this world is going to be a better place for our
grandchildren and great-grandchildren, it will be
women who make it so.

—Isabel Allende

As Jane Addams and Hull-House gained publicity, Jane was asked
to participate in a host of other city activities beyond garbage
collection. But the time involved in public activities often conflicted
with her growing family responsibilities. In 1894 Jane's favorite sister,
Mary, died. Since Mary's husband, Reverend John Linn, was unable
to care for their four children, Jane assumed that job. She paid for
the oldest, twenty-two-year-old John Linn, to continue at a seminary
in Chicago. She brought the other three—eleven-year-old Stanley,
fourteen-year-old Esther, and eighteen-year-old James Weber, who
would become Jane's future biographer—to live at Hull-House until
other plans could be arranged. She later paid college expenses for her
nephews, sometimes taking on extra lectures to earn the money for
them.

Mary's children remained closest to Jane. Jane loved the children
of her other sister, but in a more distant way. After Alice's husband,
Henry, had an affair, Alice and her daughter Marcet spent summers

Jane's brother-in-law Rev. John Linn with his son Weber.

Courtesy of the Swarthmore College Peace Collection

Jane's sister Alice holds her baby Marcet.

Wikimedia Commons

at Hull-House. Even after Henry died and Alice took over running the family bank, both women spent considerable time at Hull-House. After Alice died, Jane assumed the role of confidant and supporter for her sister's children. But Jane's full schedule sometimes strained relations. Marcet wrote: "Later, when I had come to love and fully appreciate my aunt, it seemed incredible—but the simple fact was that as a child I thought her hard and cruel."[1]

Even with a busy schedule and family responsibilities, Jane made herself available any time of day or night to everyone at Hull-House. She never feared going out alone to tend a sick neighbor, care for their children, or wash and dress dead bodies for burial. Jane and resident Julia Lathrop helped an unwed pregnant woman during labor until the doctor arrived. Everyone else shunned the woman for not being married. Whatever task she encountered, Jane brought calmness and an unusual understanding of what others needed.

Jane's empathy extended even to burglars. Her biographer and nephew James Weber wrote about one night when a man broke into Hull-House. Since "her small nephew was asleep in the next room, . . . she thought only of not awakening him. 'Don't make a noise,' she said to the burglar. Startled, he leaped for the window by which he entered. 'You'll be hurt if you go that way. . . . Go down by the stairs and let yourself out.' He did."[2]

On another occasion, Jane engaged a burglar in discussion. The man turned out to be unemployed and in need of money. Jane told him to leave but to return at nine o'clock the next morning to discuss a job. He did as he was told, and Jane found him work. For her kindness, she earned the names *Saint Jane, Miss Kind Heart,* and *Angel of Hull-House.*

POLITICS CALLS: FOR THE CHILDREN

Resident Florence Kelley encouraged Jane to ramp up her city improvement activities. Kelley and another resident, Alzina Stevens, conducted several studies that they published and distributed. Their report described street children as "ill-fed, ill-housed, ill-clothed, illiterate, and wholly untrained and unfit for any occupation." They also found that 40 percent of poor children died before age five of common diseases like diphtheria, smallpox, and scarlet fever. **Tenement houses** had only outdoor toilets, which were little more than

Jane's kindness was legendary, but she had a special fondness for children, whether relatives or Hull-House guests.

Courtesy of Rockford University

wooden benches over a hole in the ground. There were no water pipes and indoor toilets as in better homes. Kelley and Stevens reported that laborers often spent twelve to thirteen hours a day on the job, sometimes earning less than four cents an hour, a tiny sum even then.[3] They had few opportunities to move their families to better housing.

The women presented their findings to the Illinois State Board of Labor. After much prodding from the researchers—and opposition from business owners—legislators enacted the first Illinois factory law. Under the 1903 law, the state monitored sanitary conditions in **sweatshops** for the first time. The new law set the minimum age for working children at fourteen. But lawmakers, often paid off by industrial leaders, drew the line at requests for an eight-hour workday and forty-eight-hour workweek. Even when they didn't succeed, these investigations helped Jane develop theories and methods of urban social work. The foundation of the new field of social work developed from these studies.

Often Hull-House club members from the community and residents who stayed at Hull-House investigated specific social ills with other agencies. They conducted studies with the University of Chicago, the Chicago Medical Society, and the Chicago Board of Education, on which Jane served as a board member for three years. As each investigation was completed, Jane's job was to turn over the results to these outside groups and to propose solutions. Thereafter, Jane and other Hull-House women took on the job of prodding agencies into action.

Resident Gertrude Britton undertook research with the board of education to identify causes of students missing so much school. She targeted about three hundred families that she knew from her programs for more detailed study. The results indicated that children working in factories from sunup to sundown each day to help feed their families could never be expected to stay in school.[4]

From then on, child labor reform remained a lifelong cause for Jane. Her writings and lectures nationwide about child welfare brought the subject to many listeners, some for the first time. One man from Los Angeles wrote, "I have read what you had spoken at the auditorium ... about child labor. Please permit me ... to express my thanks and gratitude. . . . for the grand subject you have chosen."[5]

In 1911 Jane spoke before the Illinois State Senate about excluding children from certain jobs. At one point Jane highlighted the plight

When poor, everyone in the family worked to earn enough for food.

National Archives

Jane supported a strike by newspaper girls and boys.

National Archives

of child actors, not protected in state law: "We find that they stay up until all hours, they do not go to school the next morning, that they use foul dressing rooms, . . . and that there are many objections to children on these smaller stages."[6]

ACTION-ORIENTED JANE

No cause was off-limits to Jane. She often comforted immigrants trying to adjust to life in the United States. Many mentioned that they sent money back to families in their homelands. Middlemen convinced them that the only way to send their packages was to pay these middlemen a huge fee to do it for them. Jane thought that this was wrong. She petitioned the post office to open a Hull-House location, thereby cutting out expensive middlemen.

Another issue was bathing. Jane had seen how difficult bathing was in tenements without proper sanitation. Hull-House kept three baths in the basement for neighborhood use. Jane further pushed the board of health to open the first **public bathhouse** in Chicago. She urged the department of sanitation to force landlords to upgrade their buildings, especially with running water, toilets, and baths.

Sanitation at home or in workplaces proved a constant concern, but there was nothing that Hull-House women wouldn't tackle. After raising concerns about unsafe factory conditions, resident Florence Kelley became the state's first factory inspector in 1893, though no state law enforced her recommendations. At about the same time, resident Dr. Alice Hamilton conducted an investigation with the University of Chicago into why so many factory girls developed tuberculosis, a lung disease. During long workdays in unsanitary conditions, the illness easily spread among exhausted workers. Another resident, Julia Lathrop, pioneered study of the social ills of long workdays, poverty, and lack of education affecting children. Julia later headed the new national Children's Bureau from 1912 to 1921, the first woman chief of a US government bureau.

These women laid the groundwork for the budding field of social work. Residents Jane Addams, Julia Lathrop, and Sophonisba

Breckinridge all taught classes at the University of Chicago. Each broke new ground in areas of social sciences. They encouraged the university in 1908 to open one of the first schools to define social work as a distinct profession. Lathrop focused on protecting children and immigrants by improving housing and jails. Breckinridge conducted research that connected the impact of poverty on juvenile crime. She studied and documented the plight of working mothers, especially those who were immigrants.

They all advocated for empowering women and including immigrants and people of color in the national conversation, long dominated by White men. Resident Edith Abbott, sister of another Hull-House resident and social reformer Grace Abbott, earned the title of first dean of a university graduate school at the University of Chicago and first female dean of any graduate school in the United States. Besides establishing social work as a profession, Jane and other Hull-House women contributed to almost every aspect of city life.

Former Hull-House resident Julia Lathrop headed the federal Children's Bureau (1912–21) when this publicity poster appeared.

Library of Congress

One area of particular concern for Jane involved newsboys—and some girls—who sold newspapers on street corners. Children as young as five hawked papers at all times of day and in any weather. Most newsies, as they were called, were orphans or from families that desperately needed the penny or two earned for each paper sold. Many children suffered lung diseases and other sicknesses. No one seemed to care.

In 1903 Jane and a growing organization of several city settlements called the Federation of Settlements undertook a two-day investigation into conditions for newsies. They found that Illinois child labor laws did not cover these working children. Newsies were considered independent merchants and therefore were not included in state child labor laws.

Jane took her concerns to aldermen in the wards where most newsies lived. But these elected officials refused to buck influential newspaper owners. Frustrated, Jane spoke out on behalf of newsies: "So far, we have been unable to secure any legislative action on the subject.... The City of Chicago is careless ... towards children who are not reached by the operation of state law."[7] Her fight continued.

Did You Know?

Hull-House residents learned to tell when Jane felt down in the dumps. "Whenever she [Miss Addams] was disturbed or depressed she would move the furniture in all the rooms.... If there was no one to help her, she did it herself. Twice she fell off the tall stepladder, once breaking her arm.... It was quite customary to hear the residents at Hull-House say, 'Miss Addams is low in her mind today. She is rehanging all the pictures.'"[8]

SEVEN

MOTHER OF THE WORLD

I could see how . . . Hull-House, and Jane Addams
herself as a person, were increasingly symbols of
wide ideals, extending far beyond the boundaries
of Chicago.

—Marcet Haldeman-Julius

Always in delicate health, Jane caught typhoid fever in 1895. The
illness kept her from Hull-House for two months. During that
time, Jane stayed at Mary Rozet Smith's home. When Jane was no
longer contagious, Mary decided that she and Jane should travel to
help speed her recovery. This time, they met key contacts in England
and Russia.

Travel boosted Jane's spirits. She enjoyed learning about other
cultures and how to build understanding between nations. "We are
learning that a standard of social ethics is not attained by traveling a sequestered byway," Jane wrote to explain her philosophy of
travel.[1] In other words, Jane confirmed her thinking that she needed
to get into neighborhoods and meet local residents to truly learn
from travel.

Jane's small but impressive successes within Hull-House and the
city brought a swarm of curious guests to the settlement, some from

overseas. When English **suffragist** Ethel Snowden was about to set sail for America in 1908, a labor leader urged her to "see the greatest man in America." When she inquired who that might be, he said, "Jane Addams. . . . The greatest man in America is a woman." That same year, the *Ladies' Home Journal* listed Jane as "the foremost living woman in America."[2]

Gradually, other residents took over day-to-day duties at Hull-House. This freed Jane to dive deeper into creating change on the national level. She became a major force in three important causes of the early twentieth century: the fight for the women's vote, equal rights for Black Americans and immigrants, and eventually world peace.

WOMEN'S RIGHT TO VOTE

As a child, Jane first heard of the push for women's rights from her father. John Addams disagreed with the crushing, legally sanctioned power that fathers and husbands held over women in their families. Later, friends and teachers at Rockford Seminary had exposed her to the **suffrage** movement, the push to allow women to vote. Once at Hull-House, Jane realized how necessary a woman's vote was. In everyday life, who knew better about tainted food, infant deaths, disease-infected clothes, unsanitary housing and factories, and day-to-day decisions under the umbrella of housekeeping? Women needed the ability to decide what was best for general family welfare. That required the right to vote.

In 1907 Jane spoke before the National Suffrage Convention. She told of a small victory she had experienced with Chicago lawmakers. A measure allowing women to vote in city elections had been proposed. Ultimately the bill was defeated, but Jane considered it a victory that the issue had come up for a vote at all. Moreover, it lost by only one vote—a first. Most city planners believed that foreign women, especially, would never care to vote. "Yet the large majority are working women," Jane pointed out. "Of course they are interested." She went

Jane (right) rode and walked in several parades to push for the women's vote.
Courtesy of the Swarthmore College Peace Collection

on to reinforce the idea that women care about protection in factories, workplace safety, and the eight-hour workday: "If women are not to be treated and cared for as children, then they should have some protection of their own."[3]

Jane lectured and wrote articles about women's rights. In 1910 she closed a *Ladies' Home Journal* article with this plea: "If woman would fulfill her traditional responsibility to her own children; ... would educate and protect from danger factory children who must find their recreation on the street ... then she must bring herself to the use of the ballot."[4]

In a June 1913 article Jane reversed the argument. What if men asked women for the right to vote? "Our most valid objection ... is you are so fond of fighting—you always have been since you were little boys. You'd very likely forget that the real object of the States is to nurture and protect life, and out of sheer vainglory you would be voting away huge sums of money for battleships."[5]

Men often countered Jane's ideas with concern that having the right to vote would somehow make women unladylike. Julia Ward Howe,

Men opposed to women's suffrage formed their own group, the National Association Opposed to Women's Suffrage.

Library of Congress

author of "The Battle Hymn of the Republic," responded to New York senator Elihu Root in the *New York Times:* "Mr. Root expresses the fear that women might become ungentle and harsh if they took part in public affairs. Although Miss Addams has been engaged for many years . . . we all know that she has become neither harsh nor ungentle."[6]

The National Woman Suffrage Association (NWSA) elected Jane Addams as first vice president in 1912. The following year, she helped organize a three-day conference of the National Council of Woman Voters. The conference involved leaders of other suffrage organizations, including the NWSA, and represented four million women. Here, too, the representatives elected Jane as vice president. Their goal was to pressure Congress to propose a constitutional amendment for equal suffrage. For many years the fight continued. But for the moment, it was a big step forward simply to gather so many voices in agreement.[7]

By 1916 the woman's suffrage movement, led by women like Mrs. Suffern, with her handmade sign, had grown into a nationwide force.

Library of Congress

Jane disliked how Black people were treated, and she went out of her way to engage Black speakers at Hull-House. Not the usual leaders who advised their people to be patient, though. She asked more activist leaders to speak, like educator W. E. B. Du Bois and journalist and **anti-lynching** promoter Ida B. Wells-Barnett. Together with these and other reformers, Jane helped found the **National Association for the Advancement of Colored People (NAACP)**, which still battles prejudice today. Jane wrote articles about lynchings of innocent Black people. She spoke up at the 1912 political convention when she discovered that Black citizens from southern states were excluded from attending because of their color. Black men had gained the right to vote but were often blocked from using that right. Jane ensured that Hull-House

Reporter and civil rights activist Ida Bell Wells-Barnett became a mother and continued to write against lynching and for woman's suffrage.

Wikimedia Commons

included everyone in activities and programs, and that meant immigrants and African Americans.

Similarly, Jane promoted immigrant rights. She believed that a lack of faith in the value of all kinds of people created an unwelcoming atmosphere, although immigrants rarely experienced lynching as Black people did. She also worried that some wealthy individuals who expressed interest in helping immigrants did so with a mixture of sympathy and control, looking down on immigrants. She wanted all Americans to believe, "I am as good as you are."[8]

To give immigrants a voice, Jane helped found the **Immigrants Protective League** in 1908. Hull-House resident Grace Abbott served as its first director from 1909 to 1917. The group pushed for better work and living conditions, higher pay, and equal rights in general. The league still honors individuals from other nations who have contributed to American life in some way, whether as a nurse, a physicist, or a musician. Always loyal to the cause, Jane kept speaking and writing about Black and immigrant issues at conferences and in articles and books.

CONSCIENCE FOR PEACE DURING THE PROGRESSIVE ERA

Writers commented on Jane's broad knowledge and her ability to see all sides. Journalist Ida Tarbell called her "one of the best-read women that [she had] ever known."[9] One leader of the women's movement, Charlotte Perkins Gilman, wrote, "She could set a subject down, unprejudiced, and walk all around, allowing fairly for everyone's point of view."[10]

The more visible Jane became, the more groups chose her for leadership roles. In 1909 the National Conference of Charities and Corrections elected her as national president. The fact that the group chose a woman to lead them shocked many older members. But the men found common ground with social workers like Jane. They discussed low pay, overwork, poverty, disease, and ways to reduce these evils.

Jane used the power of the pen to further her causes. Her bestseller, *Twenty Years in Hull-House,* was published in 1911. The book sold thousands of copies, extending her influence. Her books and national reform work caught the attention of former president Theodore Roosevelt. Roosevelt agreed with Jane's concerns about immigration, the treatment of Black Americans, and labor rights. And he followed her many trips to the White House during his and President William Howard Taft's administrations on behalf of social issues.

But Roosevelt's feelings about her remained complicated. In 1907 Jane published the book *Newer Ideals of Peace,* in which she suggested that better communication between poor immigrants and labor leaders could help them work together. She proposed this joining together as a model for government leaders. She advocated responsible debate and reduction of the military. Military-minded Roosevelt disputed both ideas and sometimes grew irritated: "Don't talk to me about Jane Addams! I have always thought a lot of her, but she has just written a bad book. . . . She is all wrong about peace." But after blowing up, Roosevelt admitted, "She is a fine woman in every other way."[11]

In 1912 Roosevelt determined to run for a third term as president but needed a political party to back him. So he organized a new party with people like Jane who believed in social reform: the Progressive Party. The party was often called the Bull Moose Party to reflect Roosevelt's boast that he felt "as strong as a bull moose" and was ready to run the country again.[12]

For her part, Jane saw the new party as a chance to bring some of her ideas to the national stage. In the past, she and other social reform-

ers had avoided joining political parties. But Jane agreed with most of the issues the Progressives proposed. They promoted establishing industry standards, allowing women to vote, and protecting children and overburdened women and men. Jane swallowed her misgivings and joined Roosevelt's crusade. Yet she still felt some discomfort with Roosevelt's support for a strong military.

Promotion giveaway for the political Bull Moose Party, led by Theodore Roosevelt.

National Archives

Jane attracted large groups of women to Roosevelt's rallies. Many performed songs and called themselves Jane Addams Choruses. In 1912 Jane became a representative to the Progressive Party's convention, one of the first women to do so. In another first, Jane seconded Roosevelt's nomination in a speech before the convention. Never before had a woman been allowed on stage at a political convention. Ultimately, Roosevelt lost, giving President Woodrow Wilson a second term.

FAMILY SADNESS

Amid these many reform activities, Jane also dealt with several family issues. In 1915 Alice Addams Haldeman, Jane's remaining sister, died of cancer. Her stepbrother, George Haldeman, lived in a mental institution for several years until his death in 1918. Sadness and the ongoing care of her nieces and nephews weighed on Jane's mind constantly. Yet she carried on. Jane followed her own motto from her college days: "Always do what you are afraid to do."[13]

PEACE EFFORTS

In 1907 Jane represented women at the first National Peace Congress held in Chicago. At the Progressive convention she highlighted Roosevelt's success in settling disputes with Mexico, between Russia and Japan, and in Venezuela. Jane received thunderous applause in 1913 at New York's Carnegie Hall when she spoke about improving international communication. She left there hopeful for change. Her peace efforts caught the attention of powerful newspaper owner William Randolph Hearst, who wrote, "On the whole the reach of this woman's sympathy and understanding is beyond all comparison."[14]

On August 4, 1914, while in their Bar Harbor cottage, Jane and Mary Rozet Smith heard that war had broken out in Europe. At first, most Americans opposed involvement in the war, and President Wilson declared that the nation would stay out of it. This position assured Americans he wanted to help restore peace.

By 1915, however, stories of the brutal German invasion of Belgium began to sway public opinion to support the Allied Powers—France, England, and Russia—against the Central Powers—Germany, Austria-Hungary, Bulgaria, and the Ottoman Empire. Many men who originally opposed joining what came to be called World War I now stayed quiet. That job was left to concerned women, like Jane, to take action on behalf of peace.

In January 1915 Jane chaired the new **Woman's Peace Party**, the first independent women's peace group. The party called for a voice in foreign policy and measures to control arms and their manufacture. The meeting caught the attention of women from other nations. In April of that year, members of the Woman's Peace Party joined fifteen hundred women from twelve nations for a peace conference in The Hague, the capital city of the Netherlands. According to Jane in *Women at The Hague,* they pressed leaders for "negotiation. . . . unless the war shall continue year after year and at last be terminated through sheer exhaustion."[15]

Woman's Peace Party members were accused of meddling in affairs that didn't concern women. Within a year the mood in Washington and the nation had shifted toward war readiness. Woman's Peace Party members were called unpatriotic for not supporting the war that so many people favored. Still, the women continued to attack war as a waste of money that could be better spent on social reform.

The determined Addams met with President Wilson six times between July and December. She insisted that he seek negotiations. She visited troops in various countries to see firsthand how war affected them. She spoke again at Carnegie Hall in New York. This time didn't go as well. Her peace activities had ruined her reputation. Many felt that Jane had betrayed all soldiers by repeating the problems that men had shared on her visits. One woman wrote, "Miss Addams denies him [the soldier] the credit of his sacrifice. She strips him of honor and courage."[16]

Jane responded, "I do not mean to say that many soldiers voice that feeling."[17] Nor did she feel men lacked courage. But it was too late.

Even with the public backlash, many women agreed with Jane's stand against war. By 1916 Woman's Peace Party membership had risen to forty

Jane led a delegation of women to The Hague to discuss how to negotiate peace.

Courtesy of the Swarthmore College Peace Collection

thousand, with 165 separate offshoots nationwide. The groups marched in antiwar protests, passed out pamphlets that educated men about how to refuse military service, and hung antiwar posters. Jane testified against increased military spending before a congressional committee. Nothing worked. Wilson declared war on April 2, 1918. But Jane persisted.

Did You Know?

In 1912 Jane Addams participated in a short silent film, *Votes for Women*, produced by the National American Woman Suffrage Association (NAWSA), another group that demanded women be allowed to vote. Performers acted out how the women's vote would end sweatshops and improve conditions for families. The film wound up being a powerful fundraising and membership tool at state and local meetings for NAWSA and other suffrage organizations.

EIGHT

JANE'S LONG REACH

If the past century can't guide us, what can guide us?

—Jane Addams

Jane's peace activities during the war brought a firestorm of criticism. US, French, and British reporters attacked her in print for weeks. Even Theodore Roosevelt lashed out, calling Jane a "Bull Mouse."[1] She received many nasty letters and few supportive letters about her pleas for communication and peace. As one author wrote, she went from "'Saint Jane' to 'The Most Dangerous Woman in America.'"[2]

Hull-House neighbors who had emigrated from Central Powers nations found their loyalties questioned. Jane welcomed immigrants whom the police had harassed, and she opened the settlement for their meetings. Sometimes, police raided the offices of people suspected of reading what they called "anti-American" books and pamphlets. Jane agreed to store the books safely in her library. Some neighbors remained antiwar, while others joined the military. Hull-House still welcomed every viewpoint.

One writer described Hull-House during the war: "The distinguishing characteristics of this settlement, its unshakable tolerance [and] respect . . . for one another's firm beliefs . . . which has carried its name around the world. . . . How is it that this company preserves its ranks so . . . unbroken? The reason is their profound conviction of the worth . . . of the opinions of other people."[3]

GIVE PEACE A CHANCE

The war ended on November 11, 1918. After hearing the news Jane, with Dr. Alice Hamilton and Florence Kelley, arranged a trip to Germany. They helped local groups organize food programs to ease hunger among war victims. Jane visited battlefields to report on the devastation. At the same time, she also searched for and found the grave of her soldier nephew, John Linn. Sadly, he had died in battle and was buried in France.

The war ended with the signing of the Treaty of Versailles. Over Jane's objections, the treaty imposed on Germany a food blockade and large payments for war damages. Moreover, the former Central Powers weren't allowed membership in the proposed **League of Nations.** This group was formed to ensure that nations kept to rules of peace and cooperation. Jane liked the idea of an international league, but one that was open to all nations, including Germany. Jane feared that such harsh terms of surrender would cause German resentment that would come back to haunt the world. Sadly, her prediction came true with World War II.

For five days in May 1919, the International Women's Peace Congress in Zurich hosted a gathering of 211 women from sixteen nations, including some from the former Central Powers. Jane made special attempts to enlist non-White members. She hoped to reverse racist opinions that some suffragists took just to gain support from southern women.

Equal rights and women's suffrage activist Mary Church Terrell represented the National Association of Colored Women. Terrell remembered later, "Since I was the only delegate who gave any color to the occasion . . . , it finally dawned on me that I was representing the women of all nonwhite countries."[4]

A teacher, writer, and activist on behalf of Black people and women, Mary Church Terrell joined Black and White organizations to further these causes.

Library of Congress

The Hague International Women's Peace Congress proposed a body that included all countries. Further, "they demanded that a 'Women's Charter' be added to the peace treaty. This addition would advance equal rights for the world's citizens, especially women and minorities."[5] At the close of the meeting, delegates agreed to continue their international women's organization as a way to "further peace, internationalism, and the freedom of women."[6]

With new resolve, the congress reorganized into the Women's International League for Peace and Freedom (WILPF). The body elected Jane as president. The WILPF, which continues to this day, became the first group dedicated to nonviolence. The goal was to lobby legislators for peaceful foreign policies and social change for women and children. Their job had just begun.

After the conference Jane, Mary Rozet Smith, and Dr. Alice Hamilton traveled through other European countries to evaluate the horrors of war. The children Jane saw in war-torn areas affected her most. Throughout Germany, bony, sick children slurped "war soup," a noon meal of "wheat or rye flour, and sawdust stirred into a pint of water." This was the only meal served to the children each day.[7]

President Woodrow Wilson appointed Herbert Hoover to lead the Food Administration. In turn, Hoover asked Jane to help. She returned home to raise funds to feed starving Germans and Eastern Europeans. Once home, she was accused of being pro-German for sending to the defeated enemy goods that Americans could use. Hostile audiences now listened quietly or booed her at fundraisers. Jane tried to laugh off her unpopularity. But on some level, it must have

Jane and other women committed themselves to peace—no matter what the reaction.

National Archives

hurt. Still, she wasn't surprised that someone who opposed war, violence, and guns would be "called a traitor and a coward."[8]

In 1921 the Department of Justice put Jane on a watch list as part of their harsh "Red Hunt." The 1917 Russian Revolution had triggered fears that the **communism** imposed on its citizens would spread. Under communism, no one could own property or wealth other than what the state shared among all its citizens. Communist revolutionaries carried red flags, so suspected party members became known as "Reds." Anyone could be a suspect, especially those holding unpopular opinions—like Jane. Her nickname as the most dangerous woman in America took on added meaning.

Although never arrested, Jane sometimes felt the sting of being falsely labeled in other ways. Newspapers discredited peace women as spies. At times, Jane arrived at the Chicago Woman's Peace Party office and found spit on the mail. Other times she found the door painted with angry messages. Jane never wavered from her pursuit of justice.

ALWAYS MORE TO DO

In 1920 Congress finally passed the Nineteenth Amendment to the US Constitution, and the necessary two-thirds of the states approved it. This amendment granted women the right to vote. But prejudice against women remained in most professions. A few medical schools offered degrees to women, but hospitals often prohibited them from practicing medicine. Law schools first admitted women in the 1920s. Work for women in the legal profession was often scarce, but progress could be noted in the appointment of some judges. The arts produced such greats as author Willa Cather and painter Georgia O'Keeffe. This was just the beginning for women rising in their desired professions.

Jane didn't slow down, although ill health dogged her. In 1923 she left for a nine-month trip after the second Hague convention on international peace. Her trip stalled in Japan for an emergency operation on a breast lump. Another country, another surgery.

With more than eight million women employed in the United States, Jane saw a need for workplace protection laws. She chaired the Pan-Pacific Women's Conference in Hawaii and made plans for another meeting in 1930. Once again, nations welcomed Jane wherever she traveled.[9] Her travels took her overseas twelve times during her lifetime, amounting to one-tenth of her seventy years.

Jane continued a full schedule of writing and speaking on behalf of peace, immigration, fair labor practices, and of course, children. She signed a petition to President Calvin Coolidge to stop the sale of liquor, believing fathers drank away money that could be used to feed their hungry children.

Jane was grateful for her medical team in Japan.

National Archives

As mentioned earlier, Jane's reputation often invited criticism. To some, heading the Woman's Peace Party and WILPF had hardened her image as un-American. The real cause, however, was that she dared to challenge assumed male rights and their arguments for war, conflict, and the military. Her popularity took a hit. As one biographer wrote, "Because she was not content to allow social injustices to go unchallenged, Addams was frequently at the center of controversy."[10]

To refresh herself, Jane spent more time with Mary Rozet Smith at their restful, white cottage in Bar Harbor. Nearby were paths where Jane could hike through the pine and birch woods and pick flowers and other small treasures. Those days reminded her of how she and George had explored the woods so many years before. Jane used this quiet time to write and visit with her nieces and nephews. Niece Marcet Haldeman loved to visit. "There was often a merry note in the always significant talk, for here Aunt Jane seemed . . . more relaxed and delightful than in any other surroundings."[11]

While there, Marcet observed how Jane prepared her speeches. Jane's speeches had been legendary almost from the start of her career. Rather than being wildly emotional, Jane spoke in clear, simple terms. Her presentations showed a depth of knowledge and appreciation for her listeners. Nothing distracted from her main points. One observer added, "When you heard her speak, you felt that she knew . . . her subject on every side and not just the side of it she was presenting to you."[12]

Jane wrote her presentations by hand and often rewrote them several times to get them just right. Sometimes she cut sections with scissors. She moved the sections around until she created a new whole. Once to her liking, she pasted the parts with glue onto paper to read at gatherings. She arranged her articles the same way, since each talk usually turned into an article.

Jane's writing earned her a place in the new Society of Midland Authors, which still exists.

Courtesy of the Jane Project

Early in her career, publishers refused to print her articles. But once Hull-House and Jane's labor and peace work gained fame, they eagerly printed her writings, even though she wrote about similar themes as she had earlier. In her lifetime, Jane published eleven books and dozens of articles and pamphlets. Each year, her books earned about a thousand dollars, and her articles several hundred dollars. The small amount helped support nieces and nephews and, of course, Hull-House.

THE WORK NEVER STOPS

In 1926 Jane suffered her first heart attack. She never fully regained her health. But this didn't stop her from traveling. Each trip overseas, she met with national leaders, studied local conditions, and worked to

An older Jane continued to participate in Hull-House activities with visitors of all ages.

Courtesy of Swarthmore College Peace Collection

bring people together for peace and justice. She paid special attention to how countries treated their women and children.

As Jane aged, she campaigned for a new cause: **pensions**—that is, regular allowances for senior citizens. "If aged people had small pensions with which they could pay for their care, neighbors and relatives would often be willing to look after them."[13] She proposed this idea to President Franklin Roosevelt at age seventy-two. He eventually pushed through the Social Security Act of 1935. This system required citizens to pay some of their salary to the government program. In return, they received monthly payments when they reached a certain age.

Into her seventies, Jane began to slow down. She spent only afternoons and early evenings at Hull-House. She worked on another book at Mary Rozet Smith's Chicago home. The years were quickly slipping by, and many of Jane's closest friends and coworkers were growing old and dying. But that didn't stop Jane from working for change at home and abroad.

Jane's writings came from varied topics. In 1916 Jane Addams wrote an *Atlantic Monthly* article about a rumor that a devil baby lived at Hull-House. This fake creature displayed eleven split hooves, which were usually associated with Satan. More amazing, the baby sported pointy ears, a tiny tail, and talked from birth, often swearing. Although Jane had found similar such myths in different cultures, this one was an Italian version.

The story described a religious girl married to someone who opposed religion so much that he ripped a holy picture from the bedroom wall. He shouted that "he would quite as soon have a devil in the home as that." Supposedly this comment caused the devil to inhabit their upcoming baby. Once born, Devil Baby ran around the house cursing his father. In this version, the father caught the baby and brought him to Hull-House.

Older women first spread the fairy tale. Soon everyone seemed to think this was a good story to tell. Thousands of people spread the news by word of mouth. Before long, reporters discovered the fantastic story. Curious people called Hull-House or came to the door wanting to see the Devil Baby. Many called or offered money to get to see this odd baby. All were turned away. Disappointed, many left. Some stayed to tell their own stories of horrific experiences. Eventually, the story faded, and regular Hull-House programs resumed.[14]

Did You Know?

For years, women and some men called for Jane to run for president, even before women had the right to vote. In 1924 Chicago charity executive Charles E. Weller wrote to the *New York Times*, "Physical strength is possibly the gravest concern, but Miss Addams more than makes up for any lack of physical power by her great intellectual and spiritual powers." She never took the idea seriously.[15]

NINE

GRAND LADY OF SOCIAL REFORMS
A Fearless Run

I am a very simple person; most of the time not
right, which I am sure we all know of ourselves,
but—wanting to be.

—Jane Addams

Jane was generous almost to a fault. Throughout her forty-six years leading Hull-House, she never took a cent in salary. Besides caring for nieces and nephews, she spent most of her inheritance and earnings on Hull-House.

Jane was also known to give away gifts she received to residents and visitors. Her friend and major donor Louise deKoven Bowen wrote how Jane "always gave away everything, almost before she thanked the person for it." Knowing that Jane needed underwear, Bowen tried to end the giveaway practice. She stitched the initials *JA* into every piece for Jane. The initials didn't stop Jane: "On Christmas Day [Jane] . . . was handing out all these carefully made pieces when I bounded in. I did persuade her to keep a few in order that she might have something to wear herself."[1]

Positive opinions of Jane's activities gradually returned. Throughout her long career, Jane received many honors, some unusual for the times. In 1910 she became an honorary member of the Chicago Association of Commerce after speaking there. That was despite the group's rule to never allow women as members. Today, that rule has ended, and women participate equally.

In summer of that same year, Yale University gave Jane its first honorary degree awarded to a woman. University president Bernadotte Perrin declared Jane's work at Hull-House "the most extensive and important social settlement in the United States."[2] Jane eventually received fourteen honorary university degrees, the most of any woman at that time. The University of Illinois in Chicago later named a social work school after her.

Her nephew James Weber Linn wrote that Jane received another unusual honor. A popular magazine of the day pronounced her one of the "twelve greatest living women." A committee composed exclusively of men prepared the list. The woman who spoke for equality among all sexes—and experienced so much hatred from men   finally received a high honor from them.[3] In 1930 Jane received the Medal of Military Merit for "service to the Greek Army for her leadership during the World War." How unlikely that someone who lobbied against the military should be granted a military award![4]

Of all the recognition from institutions of learning, Jane prized the honors from Swarthmore, Rockford, and Bryn Mawr colleges the most. These awards came from women, not men. Bryn Mawr president Marion Edwards Park awarded Jane $5,000 (about $86,584 today) and said, "For the helpless, young and old, for the poor, the unlearned, the stranger, the despised, you have urged understanding and then justice."[5]

In addition to these awards, countless schools were named for Jane. Her former Cedarville school was renamed Jane Addams Elementary and was later turned into the Jane Addams Community Center.

And the remembrances continued. In 1965 a sculpture of Jane's head appeared with the dozens of famous faces displayed at the New York University Hall of Fame for Great Americans. This was the first of many sculptures molded in her honor.

NOBEL PEACE PRIZE

On December 10, 1931, calm, gray-haired Jane received formal notice that she had earned an international award, the Nobel Peace Prize. She had received a letter days before but was told to keep it a secret until the formal announcement. When she heard for sure, the seventy-one-year-old Jane lay quietly in a Baltimore hospital bed. She had just been admitted for treatment of a lump in her lung. Jane shared that year's Noble Peace Prize with Dr. Nicholas Murray Butler, who worked to strengthen international law through the Carnegie Endowment for International Peace. Jane was only the second woman and the first American woman to receive a Peace Prize, a crowning accomplishment of her international peace work.

The woman who had been shunned even by former friends ten years before had now received the highest international award. Equally important, Jane earned the award for the same thing she always did—encourage peace. Here was someone without backing from any religion, government, or other organization. Yet she achieved recognition through sheer force of her beliefs—a belief in the ability of all people to forge paths of peace and equality. Upon hearing of her honor, Jane said, "I think it is due chiefly to my presidency of the Women's International League for Peace and Freedom." And in her characteristic Jane way she added, "I will devote the money to the work of the League."[6]

Jane's lung surgery proved rough on her. Doctors refused to clear her to travel to Sweden to accept her award in person. Besides her recovery from surgery, her heart also remained too weak to travel. The US ambassador accepted the gold medal and certificate on her behalf. Since two people won the Nobel Peace Prize that year, Jane received

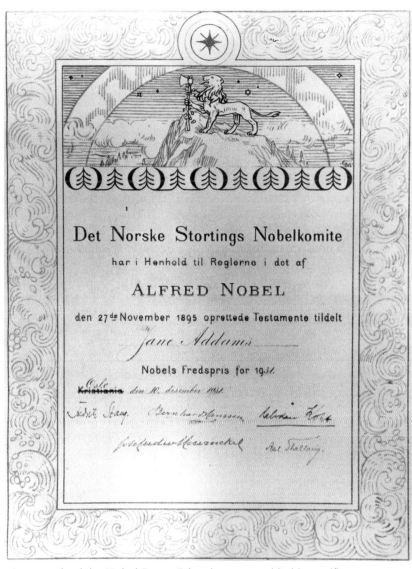

Jane received the Nobel Peace Prize that came with this certificate.

Courtesy of Rockford College

half the monetary award, $26,000 dollars, about $200,000 today. She gave her share to the WILPF. One spokesperson from the Nobel Prize Committee said, "She became the first woman of the land. . . . She did not always have public opinion with her at home or abroad, but she never surrendered her faithfulness."[7]

CELEBRATING JANE IN GRAND STYLE

Jane's mental health took a hit when her longtime friend and partner, Mary Rozet Smith, died on February 22, 1934. Mary had ordered Jane to rest in her Chicago home after a lung infection triggered another heart attack. She provided Jane with constant care, probably at the expense of her own health. When Mary caught pneumonia, she never recovered.

Jane was devastated. Sadly, she was too sick to walk downstairs for Mary's funeral. She wrote in her diary, "I suppose I could have willed my heart to stop beating, and I long to relax into doing that, but the thought of what she had been to me for so long kept me from being cowardly."[8]

Friends cared for Jane for another three months. During that time, she read. Eventually she thought of another book to write. This book would be about the life of her dear friend Julia Lathrop. With the woman's vote approved and a new book started, Jane directed her remaining energy toward peace efforts. She was determined to gain enough strength to speak at a large WILPF gathering in Washington, DC.

On May 4, 1935, Jane appeared at the twenty-fifth anniversary of the WILPF, the group she had led from 1915 through 1929. In addition to the anniversary celebration, the organization also honored Jane on her seventy-fifth birthday. Jane transmitted her speech live from inside the Washington, DC, National Broadcasting Company radio studio. Officials from around the world praised Jane to the twenty thousand WILPF members gathered at MacPherson Square, three blocks from the White House.

Every speaker celebrated Jane's "courage and [the] devotion of women who founded the league in the dark days of the World War." After the presentations ended, students marched to the White House carrying signed petitions for President Franklin Roosevelt and banners that read, "Schools, Not Battleships" and "Scholarships, Not Battleships."[9]

Jane listened to the comments and recalled those from a large birthday dinner at Chicago's Furniture Mart and her seventieth birthday dinner at Bar Harbor. On each occasion, she gave her usual modest statement: "I do not know any such person as you have described here tonight. I have never been sure that I was right; I think we all have to feel our way, step by step."[10]

"THE MOTHER OF MEN"

On May 21, 1935, three weeks after the WILPF honored Jane, she died of lung cancer. Her death brought an outpouring of affection from around the world. Illinois governor Henry Horner called her "an evening star." Educator John Dewey agreed that "she was the most human person he had ever met." A British peace seeker and WILPF member "praised her love of Life—of life as it is, not only as it might be."[11] Some compared Jane to the Catholic Saint Francis for her goodness to the poor. This tickled her nephew James Weber Linn, who knew his aunt never believed in organized religion.

As per her wishes, Jane was buried in the family plot in Cedarville. First, she lay in Hull-House's Bowen Hall. Streams of mourners filed past the coffin at a rate that at times reached fifteen hundred per hour. The outpouring of grief exceeded anything ever seen before in Chicago.

A funeral service was held in the main court of Hull-House. The courtyard filled well before the service started. Police closed nearby streets to traffic. University of Chicago chaplain Dr. Charles Gilkey and Jane's longtime friend, the religious leader Dr. Graham Taylor, led the service. Children from the Hull-House Music School played and sang.

Jane's grave marker celebrated her two most important achievements: Hull-House and the WIPLF.

Courtesy of Rockford University

After the service, police escorted the horse and carriage carrying the coffin, an honor given only to great leaders and public servants. A police officer on the street asked whether it was Jane's coffin that the horse was pulling. When the driver said yes, the officer stopped all traffic and hushed the onlookers. Then he said, "She goes in peace." The mention of peace would have pleased Jane.[12]

The train with Jane's body arrived at the Cedarville train station established by her father. Friends and family waited for her at the Cedarville Cemetery. Jane always considered her two greatest achievements to be Hull-House and the Women's International League for Peace and Freedom. Both were engraved on her tombstone.

Jane worked hard to better this world. The ideals that made her dangerous live on to this day. And the life of Jane Addams, a devoted woman of peace, brings up an age-old question: How do you remain true to peace if others refuse to play by the same rules? What will you do to further the causes of peace and social justice?

Did You Know?

Jane was offered a resting place next to President Woodrow Wilson in the Washington National Cathedral. True to herself, Jane preferred to be buried with her family.

Timeline

1860   *September 6:* Jane is born in Cedarville, Illinois, the eighth child of Sarah Weber Addams and John Huy Addams.

1863   *January 14:* Jane's mother dies in childbirth. Her oldest sister Mary Catherine, age seventeen, and the family nurse, Polly Beer, take over raising the youngest Addamses: Jane, age two; Sarah Alice, age nine; and John Weber, age ten.

1864   Jane, age four, becomes sick with a form of spinal tuberculosis, which causes a curved spine and lifelong pain.

1867   *Fall:* Jane starts school at Cedarville Public School, where she's known as Jennie.

1868   *November 17:* John Addams marries the widow Anna Hostetter Haldeman of Freeport, Illinois, bringing seven-year-old George with her and son Henry, who stayed at school.

1877   *September:* Jane enters Rockford Female Seminary, her first time living away from home. There Jane meets and befriends Ellen Gates Starr, her future Hull-House cofounder.

1879   *Summer:* Jane becomes editor and writer of the *Rockford Seminary Magazine.*

1881   *June 22:* Jane graduates from Rockford Female Seminary as valedictorian.

        Jane's father dies from a burst appendix, leaving Jane with lasting sadness.

        Jane goes to the Woman's Medical College of Pennsylvania and passes her exams but leaves due to spine problems and nervous exhaustion.

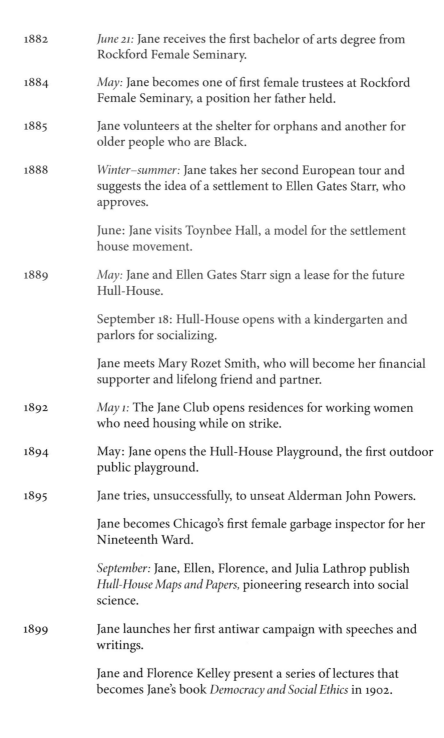

1882	*June 21:* Jane receives the first bachelor of arts degree from Rockford Female Seminary.
1884	*May:* Jane becomes one of first female trustees at Rockford Female Seminary, a position her father held.
1885	Jane volunteers at the shelter for orphans and another for older people who are Black.
1888	*Winter–summer:* Jane takes her second European tour and suggests the idea of a settlement to Ellen Gates Starr, who approves.
	June: Jane visits Toynbee Hall, a model for the settlement house movement.
1889	*May:* Jane and Ellen Gates Starr sign a lease for the future Hull-House.
	September 18: Hull-House opens with a kindergarten and parlors for socializing.
	Jane meets Mary Rozet Smith, who will become her financial supporter and lifelong friend and partner.
1892	*May 1:* The Jane Club opens residences for working women who need housing while on strike.
1894	May: Jane opens the Hull-House Playground, the first outdoor public playground.
1895	Jane tries, unsuccessfully, to unseat Alderman John Powers.
	Jane becomes Chicago's first female garbage inspector for her Nineteenth Ward.
	September: Jane, Ellen, Florence, and Julia Lathrop publish *Hull-House Maps and Papers,* pioneering research into social science.
1899	Jane launches her first antiwar campaign with speeches and writings.
	Jane and Florence Kelley present a series of lectures that becomes Jane's book *Democracy and Social Ethics* in 1902.

1903	*Fall:* Jane is elected vice president of the new National Women's Trade Union.
1905–8	Jane serves as a member of the Chicago Board of Education.
1907:	Macmillan publishes Jane's *Newer Ideals of Peace,* and Theodore Roosevelt responds, "Foolish Jane."
	June: The new League for the Protection of Immigrants chooses Jane as its second vice president.
1909	*June:* Jane becomes the first woman president of the National Conference of Charities and Corrections, later known as the National Conference of Social Work.
1910	Jane opens Hull-House to relieve workers out of work for their strike against the Hart, Schaffner, and Marx Garment Company.
	November: Macmillan publishes *Twenty Years at Hull House,* which becomes Jane's most autobiographical and popular book.
1911–14	Jane serves as vice president of the National American Woman Suffrage Association and speaks out on behalf of the women's vote.
1912	*January:* Jane helps found the National Association for the Advancement of Colored People.
1913	*June:* The state of Illinois grants the women's vote.
1915	*January:* War in Europe causes Jane and three thousand women to form the Woman's Peace Party with Jane as president.
	March 10: Janes's sister Sarah Alice Haldeman dies.
	April–May: Jane and peace activists organize the International Congress of Women in The Hague. Jane travels to warring countries.
	July 9: Jane gives a rousing speech for peace at Carnegie Hall that causes offense.

1919	*May:* The Women's International League for Peace and Freedom is established, with Jane as president. Jane investigates food conditions in Germany and other war-torn nations.
1920	Jane is a founding member of the American Civil Liberties Union (ACLU).
1931	*December:* Jane becomes the first American woman to receive the Nobel Peace Prize and donates her prize to the Women's International League for Peace and Freedom.
1934	*February 22:* Jane's longtime partner, Mary Rozet Smith, dies from pneumonia while tending Jane, who is recovering from a second heart attack.
1935:	*May 2:* First Lady Eleanor Roosevelt and twelve hundred guests in Washington, DC, mark the twentieth anniversary of the Women's International League and honor its founder and honorary president, Jane.
	May 18: Surgeons operate on Jane in Chicago to treat cancer.
	May 21: Jane Addams dies.

Glossary

alderman: elected official who represents an area of the city

anti-lynching: opposing the hanging of anyone without legal approval or process

appendix: thin, four-inch-long tube in the lower-right area of the abdomen

communism: belief that no one should own property as an individual

depression: an extreme feeling of sadness that lasts longer than usual and interferes with daily activities

Immigrants Protective League: group founded by Jane Addams and others to gain equal rights for newcomers to the United States

League of Nations: first worldwide organization dedicated to international peace and cooperation

lobby: influence or sway of a certain position

miller: someone who runs machinery to grind raw materials, usually grains

missionaries: religious people, in this case, Christians, sent to remote areas to promote their faith and provide services, such as education, social justice, and healthcare

National Association for the Advancement of Colored People (NAACP): organization founded by Jane Addams and Ida B. Wells-Barnett and others to push for Black equality and anti-lynching laws

National Confectionary Association: group focused on making and distributing sweet foods, or confections

National Conference of Charities: group founded by Jane Addams and other social workers that elected her as president

opium: drug made from the poppy plant that was once thought safe for nervous disorders but has since been banned for easily causing someone to become addicted

pension: allowance for older citizens once they stop working outside the home

phrenologist: now considered a fake doctor who measures the skull to predict mental traits

physiology: study of the body and its functions

Pott's disease: a form of tuberculosis that does not spread to others; Jane Addams suffered from this disease, which caused her pain and made her spine curve

Progressive Era: time when social reformers concentrated on issues affecting everyday Americans—worker, Black, and immigrant rights; women's voting rights; child labor

public bathhouse: a place outside the home or apartment where people could bathe

rabble-rouser: a rebel; someone who excites the emotions of people about an issue

rhetoric: study of language and its usage

seminary: a school providing education in theology or religion

settlement house: term used to describe a home in a poor city area where free educational and cultural activities were offered to neighbors and where volunteers lived and shared ideas

social work: organized activities that improve community social services: Jane Addams helped transform this work into a formal profession

strike: workers stopping work to protest employer demands

suffrage: right to vote in public elections, something women didn't have until 1921

suffragist: women who advocate for the woman's vote

sweatshops: crowded, unsanitary, and unsafe workplaces where the poor toiled for long hours for little pay

taxidermy: art of preserving an animal body by mounting or stuffing it

tenement house: apartment building with poor conditions

tuberculosis: serious lung disease that causes coughing, can spread to other parts of the body, and is transmitted through the air.

typhoid fever: a serious bacterial infection

Underground Railroad: network of safe houses where escaped slaves found shelter on their way to freedom farther north

union: organization of workers who call for better wages and working conditions as one voice

valedictorian: student who ranked highest in a graduating class

Woman's Peace Party: first independent women's peace group that elected Jane Addams as chairwoman in 1915

Acknowledgments

This book was written during the COVID-19 pandemic. As an author, I prefer in-person interviews and research. Yet the pandemic required me to stay safely at home as libraries and historical societies closed their doors to researchers. Luckily, even I, someone who growls at the computer regularly, discovered the value of finding trusted sources online. Kind phone contacts sent me amazing research digitally. The phone plus internet and digital transmissions saved the day.

Some people who particularly helped me were Jim Bade of the Cedarville Area Historical Society; Diane Fagen and Joanna Mladic, library archivists at the Rockford University Archives; Kristin Lems, an educator, a performing songwriter, and a playwright of *Saint June and the Wicked Wicks*; and Rachel Mattson of the Swarthmore College Peace Collection.

I also want to give a shout-out to the great team at Ohio University Press. Thanks to Sally Welch for keeping the details straight, Jeffrey Kallet for top-notch promotions, and a special thanks to acquisitions editor in chief, Ricky Huard, and his new editor, Tyler Balli, and series editor, Michelle Houts, for taking another chance on me and for answering my endless questions, and I can't forget Laura André for adding her artistic skills.

My family played a role too. Professors Dena Epstein Targ and Harry Targ offered contacts and books, and Richard Brill provided in-house technical skills. Of course, I always thank our daughter, Alison Brill, for her constant support.

Notes

AUTHOR'S NOTE

1. Quoted in Marlene Targ Brill, *Let Women Vote* (Brookfield, CT: Millbrook Press, 1996), 16.
2. Genesis 3:16 (King James Version).

CHAPTER ONE:
SETTING THE STAGE FOR MUCH-NEEDED MISCHIEF MAKING

Epigraph: Jane Addams, "Democracy and Social Ethics: Defending Care Ethics," quoted in *Kids as Agents of Social Change* (Jane Addams Peace Association, 2019), 1, https://www.janeaddamschildrensbookaward .org/kids-as-agents-of-social-change/.
1. Jane Addams, *Twenty Years at Hull House,* foreword by Henry Steele Commager (New York: New American Library, 1960), xii.
2. Edith Abbott, *The Tenements of Chicago, 1908–1935* (Chicago: University of Chicago Press, 1936), 16.
3. Addams, *Twenty Years,* 81.

CHAPTER TWO: NOT YOUR TRADITIONAL GIRL

Epigraph: Jane Addams, *Rockford Seminary Magazine,* Rockford Female Seminary, 1869–1870.
1. Gioia Diliberto, *A Useful Woman: The Early Life of Jane Addams* (New York: Scribner, 1999), 25.
2. Paul E. Fry, *Generous Spirit: The Life of Mary Fry* (self-published, 2003), 22.
3. Diliberto, *A Useful Woman,* 25.
4. Diliberto, *A Useful Woman,* 29.
5. Diliberto, *A Useful Woman,* 29.
6. James Weber Linn, *Jane Addams: A Biography* (Urbana: University of Illinois Press, 2000), 22.

7. Linn, *Jane Addams,* 22.
8. Diliberto, *A Useful Woman,* 40.
9. John Addams Obituary, "Dead. Hon. John H. Addams of Cedarville, Died at Green Bay, Wisconsin, on Wednesday Last," cited in Jane Addams, *Twenty Years at Hull-House,* foreword by Henry Steele Commager (New York: New American Library, 1960), 39.
10. Addams, *Twenty Years,* 20.
11. Addams, *Twenty Years,* 20.
12. Addams, *Twenty Years,* 22.
13. Addams, *Twenty Years,* 24.
14. Linn, *Jane Addams,* 33.
15. Judith Bloom Fradin and Dennis Brindell Fradin, *Jane Addams: Champion of Democracy* (New York: Clarion, 2006), 24.

CHAPTER THREE: ROADMAP FOR THE FUTURE: TROUBLEMAKER

Epigraph: Jane Addams, *Twenty Years at Hull-House,* foreword by Henry Steele Commager (New York: New American Library, 1960), 47.
1. Mrs. Karl [Dorothy] Detzer collection, Jane Addams Memorial Collection, University of Illinois at Chicago Circle.
2. James Weber Linn, *Jane Addams: A Biography* (Urbana: University of Illinois Press, 2000), 42.
3. Gioia Diliberto, *A Useful Woman: The Early Life of Jane Addams* (New York: Scribner, 1999), 64.
4. Linn, *Jane Addams,* 49.
5. Diliberto, *A Useful Woman,* 63.
6. Linn, *Jane Addams,* 47.
7. Linn, *Jane Addams,* 44.
8. Diliberto, *A Useful Woman,* 71.
9. Addams, *Twenty Years,* 53.
10. Addams, *Twenty Years,* 197.

CHAPTER FOUR: FALSE STARTS

Epigraph: Jane Addams, *Twenty Years at Hull-House,* foreword by Henry Steele Commager (New York: New American Library, 1960), 100.
1. Addams, *Twenty Years,* 57.
2. Addams, *Twenty Years,* 60.
3. James Weber Linn, *Jane Addams: A Biography* (Urbana: University of Illinois Press, 2000), 74.
4. Gioia Diliberto, *A Useful Woman: The Early Life of Jane Addams* (New York: Scribner, 1999), 119.

5. Marcet Haldeman-Julius, *Jane Addams as I Knew Her* (Girard, KS: Haldeman-Julius Publications, 1936), 5.

6. Diliberto, *A Useful Woman*, 118–19.

7. Jeffrey Scheuer, *Legacy of Light: University Settlement's First Century*, excerpted in "Origins of the Settlement House Movement," VCU Libraries Social Welfare History Project, accessed February 1, 2024, https://socialwelfare.library.vcu.edu/settlement-houses/origins-of-the-settlement-house-movement/.

CHAPTER FIVE: HEAD REBEL-ROUSER

Epigraph: "Address of Miss Jane Addams," February 23, 1903, address to Chicago's Union League Club, in Jane Addams Digital Edition, the Jane Addams Papers Project, Ramapo College, https://digital.janeaddams.ramapo.edu/items/show/1174.

1. Marcet Haldeman-Julius, *Jane Addams as I Knew Her* (Girard, KS: Haldeman-Julius Publications, 1936), 1.

2. Dorothea Moore, "A Day at Hull-House," *American Journal of Sociology* 11, no. 5 (March 1897): 632–40.

3. James Weber Linn, *Jane Addams: A Biography* (Urbana: University of Illinois Press, 2000), 115.

4. Haldeman-Julius, *Jane Addams*, 1.

5. Jane Addams, *Twenty Years at Hull House*, foreword by Henry Steele Commager (New York: New American Library, 1960), xi.

6. See "How Was Hull-House Funded?" at "FAQ: Jane Addams and Hull-House," Jane Addams Hull-House Museum (website), accessed January 14, 2022, https://www.hullhousemuseum.org/faq.

7. Addams, *Twenty Years*, xi.

8. Haldeman-Julius, *Jane Addams*, 5.

9. Cornelia Meigs, *Jane Addams: Pioneer for Social Justice* (Boston: Little, Brown, 1970), 145, quoted in Rodger Streitmatter, *Outlaw Marriages: The Hidden Stories of Fifteen Extraordinary Same-Sex Couples* (Boston: Beacon Press, 2012), 35–36.

10. Linn, *Jane Addams*, 125.

11. *First Report of the Labor Museum at Hull House, Chicago, 1901–1902* (privately printed, 1902), 13, in Jane Addams Digital Edition, the Jane Addams Papers Project, Ramapo College, https://digital.janeaddams.ramapo.edu/items/show/1189.

12. Hilda Satt Polacheck, *I Came a Stranger: The Story of a Hull-House Girl* (Urbana: University of Illinois Press, 1989), 65.

13. Polacheck, *I Came a Stranger*, 63–64.

14. Addams, *Twenty Years*, 285.

15. Louise W. Knight, *Citizen: Jane Addams and the Struggle for Democracy* (Chicago: University of Chicago Press, 2005), 319.

16. Judith Bloom Fradin and Dennis Brindell Fradin, *Jane Addams: Champion of Democracy* (New York: Clarion, 2006), 93.

17. See "Who Was Mary Rozet Smith?" at "FAQ: Jane Addams and Hull-House," Jane Addams Hull-House Museum (website), accessed January 14, 2022, https://www.hullhousemuseum.org/faq.

18. "Pioneer Patron of Hull House, Mary Smith Dies," *Chicago Daily Tribune,* February 24, 1934, 20.

CHAPTER SIX: MORE GOOD TROUBLE

Epigraph: Isabel Allende, interview with Tavis Smiley, PBS, May 13, 2010, 12:00–12:30 p.m.

1. Marcet Haldeman-Julius, *Jane Addams as I Knew Her* (Girard, KS: Haldeman-Julius Publications, 1936), 6.

2. James Weber Linn, *Jane Addams: A Biography* (Urbana: University of Illinois Press, 2000), 114.

3. *Hull-House Maps and Papers,* cited in Jeff Link, "Jane Addams Hull-House Museum: Inside the Home of a Legendary Social Reformer and Play Advocate," Goric, December 11, 2017, https://goric.com/jane-addams -hull-house-museum.

4. Jane Addams, *Twenty Years at Hull-House,* foreword by Henry Steele Commager (New York: New American Library, 1960), 212.

5. Henry Joseph Warren to Jane Addams, May 4, 1902, Jane Addams Papers, Series 1, Supplement, Peace Collection, Swarthmore College Special Collections.

6. "Addams Statement on Illinois State Senate Bill 233, March 8, 1911," Jane Addams: Right to Childhood, http://njdigitalhistory.org/jane-addams -child-labor/index.php/addams-statement-on-illinois-state-senate-bill -233-march-8-1911/.

7. Stacy Linn, "Jane Addams and the News Babies of Chicago," *Jane Addams Papers* (blog), April 3, 2007, https://janeaddams.ramapo.edu/2017 /04/jane-addams-and-the-news-babies-of-chicago/.

8. Jean Bethke Elshtain, *Jane Addams and the Dream of Democracy* (New York: Basic Books, 2002), 150–51.

CHAPTER SEVEN: MOTHER OF THE WORLD

Epigraph: Marcet Haldeman-Julius, *Jane Addams as I Knew Her* (Girard, KS: Haldeman-Julius Publications, 1936), 27.

1. Jane Addams, *Woman's Journal* 38 (March 2, 1907): 26, in Jane Addams Digital Edition, the Jane Addams Papers Project, Ramapo College, https://digital.janeaddams.ramapo.edu/items/show/5977.

2. Neil Lanctot, *The Approaching Storm: Roosevelt, Wilson, Adams and Their Clash over America's Future* (New York: Riverhead Books, 2021), 8.

3. Jane Addams, "The Campaign for Municipal Suffrage, February 17, 1907," in Jane Addams Digital Edition, the Jane Addams Papers Project, Ramapo College, https:digital.janeaddams.ramapo.edu/items/show/5977.

4. Jane Addams, "Both Sides of Live Questions Why Women Should Vote," *Ladies' Home Journal,* January 1910, 22, in Jane Addams Digital Edition, the Jane Addams Papers Project, Ramapo College, https://digital.janeaddams.ramapo.edu/items/show/6155.

5. Jane Addams, "If Men Were Seeking the Franchise," *Ladies' Home Journal,* June 1913, 1, Jane Addams Digital Edition, the Jane Addams Papers Project, Ramapo College, https://digital.janeaddams.ramapo.edu/items/show/8978.

6. Julia Ward Howe, letter to the editor, "Jane Addams on Suffrage," *New York Times,* March 20, 1909.

7. "To Put Suffrage in Constitution: Representatives of 4,000,000 Women Voters Plan for National Amendment, Conferring in Washington They Urge the House to Create a Woman Suffrage Committee—Pressure on Democrats," *New York Times,* August 14, 1913, 6.

8. Jane Addams, "What Is the Greatest Menace to Twentieth Century Progress?," *Unity,* April 4, 1901, 71.

9. Lanctot, *Approaching Storm,* 9.

10. Lanctot, *Approaching Storm,* 20.

11. Judith Bloom Fradin and Dennis Brindell Fradin, *Jane Addams: Champion of Democracy* (New York: Clarion, 2006), 121.

12. Jane Addams, *The Second Twenty Years at Hull-House, September 1909 to September 1929, with a Record of a Growing Consciousness* (New York: Macmillan, 1930), 33–34.

13. James Weber Linn, *Jane Addams: A Biography* (Urbana: University of Illinois Press, 2000), 294.

14. Ed L. Keen, "Peace Congress Picks Jane Addams as Chairman," United Press, April 28, 1915, UPI Archives, https://www.upi.com/Archives/1915/04/28/Peace-Congress-picks-Jane-Addams-as-chairman/8693168210471/.

15. Marlene Targ Brill, *Women for Peace* (New York: Franklin Watts, 1997), 67.

16. Richard Harding Davis, "An Insult to War," *New York Times,* July 13, 1915, 10.

17. John J. Halsey, "What Miss Addams Meant," *New York Times*, August 18, 1915, 10.

CHAPTER EIGHT: JANE'S LONG REACH

Epigraph: Jane Addams, "One Menace to the Century," *Unity*, April 4, 1901, 71–72.

1. Rutherford H. Platt, "Ukraine: A Test for World Peace Advocates," *Daily Hampshire Gazette*, March 3, 2022.
2. Rich Wilson, "Jane Addams (1860–1935)," Profiles of Ten LGBT Activists for Social Justice, Outhistory: It's About Time! (website), December 10, 2013, https://outhistory.org/exhibits/show/raisedvoicesamongprettymanners /raisedvoicesjaneaddams.
3. Jane Addams, *The Second Twenty Years at Hull-House, September 1909 to September 1929, with a Record of a Growing Consciousness* (New York: Macmillan 1930), 142–43.
4. Harriet Hyman Alonso, *Peace as a Women's Issue* (Syracuse, NY: Syracuse University Press, 1993), 38.
5. Marlene Targ Brill, *Women for Peace* (New York: Franklin Watts, 1997), 72.
6. Alonso, *Peace*, 83.
7. James Weber Linn, *Jane Addams: A Biography* (Urbana: University of Illinois Press, 2000), 345.
8. Linn, *Jane Addams*, 349.
9. Linn, *Jane Addams*, 335.
10. Sherry Shepler and Anne Mattina, "The Revolt against War: The Rhetorical Challenge to the Patriarchy," *Communication Quarterly* 47, no. 2 (Spring 1999): 151.
11. Marcet Haldeman-Julius, *Jane Addams as I Knew Her* (Girard, KS: Haldeman-Julius Publications, 1936), 14.
12. Linn, *Jane Addams*, 117.
13. Linn, *Jane Addams*, 403.
14. Addams, *Second Twenty Years*; Jane Addams, "The Devil Baby at Hull-House," *The Atlantic*, October 1916, 49–70.
15. Charles F. Weller, "Jane Addams for President," *New York Times*, March 2, 1924, 161.

CHAPTER NINE: A FEARLESS RUN

Epigraph: James Weber Linn, *Jane Addams: A Biography* (Urbana: University of Illinois Press, 2000), 416.

1. Louise deKoven Bowen, *Open Windows: Stories of People and Places* (Chicago: Seymour, 1946), 219–20.
2. Sherry Shepler and Anne Mattina, "Paying the Price for Pacifism: The Press's Rhetorical Shift from 'Saint Jane' to the Most Dangerous Woman in America," *Feminist Formations* 24, no. 1 (Spring 2012), 5.
3. "Jane Addams," *New York Times,* May 23, 1935, 22.
4. "Greece Honors Jane Addams," *New York Times,* March 18, 1930, 6.
5. James Weber Linn, *Jane Addams: A Biography* (Urbana: University of Illinois Press, 2000), 387.
6. Mildred Scott Olmsted, "Jane Addam's Work," *New York Times,* November 13, 1965, 28.
7. Eunice Fuller Barnard, "Jane Addams: Bold Crusader for Peace," *New York Times,* 112.
8. Linn, *Jane Addams,* 407–8.
9. "Five Nations Unite in Plea for Peace," *New York Times,* May 4, 1935, 14.
10. Linn, *Jane Addams,* 416.
11. Louise Knight, *Spirit in Action* (New York: W. W. Norton, 2010), 268.
12. Linn, *Jane Addams,* 423.

Bibliography

BOOKS

Books for Older Readers

Addams, Jane. *Newer Ideals of Peace.* With an introduction by Berenice A. Carroll and Clinton Fink. Chicago: University of Illinois Press, 2007.

Alonso, Harriet Hyman. *Peace as a Women's Issue.* Syracuse, NY: Syracuse University Press, 1993.

Beam, Ronald. *Cedarville's Jane Addams: Her Early Influences.* Revised by Paul Fry. Cedarville, IL: Cedarville Area Historical Society, 2007. Originally published in 1966.

Bobick, Ruth. *Six Remarkable Hull-House Women.* Portsmouth, NH: Peter E. Randall, 2015.

Diliberto, Gioia. *A Useful Woman: The Early Life of Jane Addams.* New York: Scribner, 1999.

Elshtain, Jean Bethke. *Jane Addams and the Dream of American Democracy.* New York: Basic Books, 2002.

Haldeman-Julius, Marcet. *Jane Addams as I Knew Her.* Girard, KS: Haldeman-Julius Publications, 1936.

Knight, Louise. *Jane Addams: Spirit in Action.* New York: W.W. Norton, 2010.

Lanctot, Neil. *The Approaching Storm: Roosevelt, Wilson, Addams and Their Clash Over America's Future.* New York: Riverhead Books, 2021.

Linn, James Weber. *Jane Addams: A Biography.* Urbana: University of Illinois Press, 2000.

Metzger, Janice. *What Would Jane Say?* Chicago: Lake Claremont, 2009.

Polacheck, Hilda Satt. *I Came a Stranger: The Story of a Hull-House Girl.* Urbana: University of Illinois Press, 1989.

Streitmatter, Rodger. *Outlaw Marriages: The Hidden Stories of Fifteen Extraordinary Same-Sex Couples.* Boston: Beacon Press, 2012.

Books for Younger Readers

Brill, Marlene Targ. *Let Women Vote.* Brookfield, CT: Millbrook, 1996. Middle grade.

Brill, Marlene Targ. *Women for Peace.* New York: Franklin Watts, 1997. Young adult.

Fradin, Judith Bloom, and Dennis Brindell Fradin. *Jane Addams: Champion of Democracy.* New York: Clarion, 2006. Young adult.

Hovde, Jane. *Jane Addams.* New York: Facts on File, 1989. Young adult.

Rappaport, Doreen. *American Women: Their Lives in Their Words.* New York: Thomas Y. Crowell, 1990. Young adult.

Slade, Suzanne. *Dangerous Jane.* Atlanta: Peachtree, 2017. Picture book.

Stone, Tanya Lee. *The House That Jane Built: A Story about Jane Addams.* New York: Henry Holt, 2015. Picture book.

Wheeler, Leslie. *Jane Addams.* Englewood Cliffs, NJ: Silver Burdett, 1990. Young adult.

Books by Jane Addams

Democracy and Social Ethics. New York: Macmillan, 1902. Reprinted, Urbana: University of Illinois Press, 2002.

The Excellent Becomes the Permanent. New York: Macmillan, 1932.

Forty Years at Hull-House: Including "Twenty Years at Hull-House" and "The Second Twenty Years at Hull-House." With an afterword by Lillian Wald. New York: Macmillan, 1935.

The Long Road of Woman's Memory. New York: Macmillan, 1916. Reprinted, Urbana: University of Illinois Press, 2002.

My Friend, Julia Lathrop. New York: Macmillan, 1935. Reprinted, Urbana: University of Illinois Press, 2004.

A New Conscience and an Ancient Evil. New York: Macmillan, 1912. Reprinted, Urbana: University of Illinois Press, 2002.

Newer Ideals of Peace. New York: Macmillan, 1907. Reprinted, Urbana: University of Illinois Press, 2007.

Peace and Bread in Time of War. New York: Macmillan, 1922. Reprinted, Urbana: University of Illinois Press, 2002.

The Second Twenty Years at Hull-House, September 1909 to September 1929, with a Record of a Growing Consciousness. New York: Macmillan, 1930.

The Spirit of Youth and the City Streets. New York: Macmillan, 1909. Reprinted, Urbana: University of Illinois Press, 2001.

Twenty Years at Hull-House. Foreword by Henry Steele Commager. New York: New American Library, 1960.

FILMS AND VIDEOS

Lems, Kristin, writer and producer. *St. Jane and the Wicked Wicks* (historical musical). YouTube video, 1:58:27, September 21, 2021. https://www.youtube.com/watch?v=eLVj5waLTf8.

Cedarville Area Historical Society, Cedarville, IL. Museum with significant Jane Addams and Addams family memorabilia.

Jane Addams Collection, 1894–1919. The Hanna Holborn Gray Special Collections Research Center. University of Chicago Library. https://www.lib.uchicago.edu/e/scrc/findingaids/view.php?eadid=ICU.SPCL.ADDAMSJ. Focuses on correspondence 1894–1919.

Jane Addams Digital Edition. The Jane Addams Papers Project. Ramapo College. https://digital.janeaddams.ramapo.edu/collection-tree. Currently focuses on correspondence and writings (excluding books) written between 1901 and 1935.

Jane Addams and Hull-House Collection. Howard Colman Library. Rockford University. Rockford, IL. Large collection of photos, diaries, and other documents.

Jane Addams Hull-House Museum, Chicago. The museum has a large collection of letters and photos.

Peace Collection. Swarthmore College Special Collections. http://swarthmore.edu/library/peace. Includes correspondence, Rockford Seminary notebooks, diaries, engagement calendars, writings, and speeches by and about Addams, passports, visiting cards, reviews of her books, reference files, death notices, condolences, descriptions of memorial services, photographs, the Nobel Peace Prize medal, memorabilia, and a very large quantity of mounted clippings (1892–1935) about Addams.

BIOGRAPHIES FOR YOUNG READERS

MICHELLE HOUTS, SERIES EDITOR

Michelle Houts, *Kammie on First: Baseball's Dottie Kamenshek*

Julie K. Rubini, *Missing Millie Benson: The Secret Case of the Nancy Drew Ghostwriter and Journalist*

Nancy Roe Pimm, *The Jerrie Mock Story: The First Woman to Fly Solo around the World*

Julie K. Rubini, *Virginia Hamilton: America's Storyteller*

Michelle Houts, *Count the Wings: The Life and Art of Charley Harper*

Marlene Targ Brill, *Dolores Huerta Stands Strong: The Woman Who Demanded Justice*

Nancy Roe Pimm, *Smoky, the Dog That Saved My Life: The Bill Wynne Story*

Julie K. Rubini, *Eye to Eye: Sports Journalist Christine Brennan*

Scott H. Longert, *Cy Young: An American Baseball Hero*

Andrew Speno, *The Many Lives of Eddie Rickenbacker*

Alysa Landry, *Thomas H. Begay and the Navajo Code Talkers*

Marlene Targ Brill, *Jane Addams: The Most Dangerous Woman in America*